GUIDE+MAP **MALLORCA**

SERRA DE
TRAMUNTANA

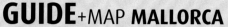

WORLD HERITAGE SITE **UNESCO** 2011

- VILLAGES
- COVES AND BEACHES
- PLACES OF INTEREST
- CAR TOURS
- WALKS
- PRACTICAL GUIDE

TRIANGLE ▼ BOOKS

VILLAGES

The chapter dedicated to the towns and villages of the Serra de Tramuntana include the explanation of 29 places spread between 20 districts that make up the county of the Mallorca mountain, some of which also take part in the neighbouring county of Raiguer. We come across very different towns, from large urban conglomerations to small villages rooted and integrated in the essence of the mountain, as well as coastal tourist centres.

➜ P. 15

ANDRATX ➜ P. 17

PORT D'ANDRATX AND CAMP DE MART ➜ P. 18

S'ARRACÓ ➜ P. 20

SANT ELM ➜ P. 21

ESTELLENCS ➜ P. 22

BANYALBUFAR ➜ P. 25

CALVIÀ ➜ P. 26

ES CAPDELLÀ ➜ P. 28

GALILEA ➜ P. 29

PUIGPUNYENT ➜ P. 29

ESPORLES ➜ P. 30

COVES
AND BEACHES

We suggest you discover the coastline of the Serra de Tramuntana from the coves and beaches suitable for bathing. They are spots that can be visited all year round, always surrounded by delightful and, sometimes, captivating scenery, between mountains and high cliffs. We can come across well-known and busy beaches in summer or more solitary corners, far from urbanisations, but also visited by yachts and boats. ➜ P. 69

CALA D'EGOS ➜ P. 70

CALA EN BASSET ➜ P. 70

BEACH OF SANT ELM AND CALA CONILLS ➜ P. 71

PLACES OF INTEREST

We have chosen eleven points of interest that are well worth visiting; all of them —except Sa Dragonera and Puig de Maria— have access by vehicle. They are mainly old monasteries or sanctuaries but also houses of *possessions*, with their gardens, converted into museums.

→ P. 87

LA TRAPA AND SA DRAGONERA → P. 88

TALAIA DE SES ÀNIMES → P. 90

LA CARTOIXA → P. 91

GARDENS OF RAIXA → P. 94

GARDENS OF ALFÀBIA → P. 97

LA GRANJA → P. 99

MIRAMAR → P. 101

SON MARROIG → P. 103

SANCTUARY OF LLUC → P. 107

PUIG DE MARIA → P. 108

CAP DE FORMENTOR → P. 109

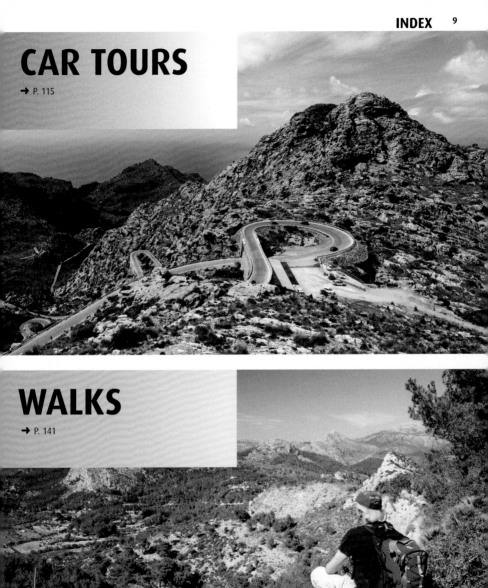

CAR TOURS
➜ P. 115

WALKS
➜ P. 141

Carrer de la Rectoria, Valldemossa

SERRA DE TRAMUNTANA

The Serra de Tramuntana was declared a UNESCO World Heritage Site in the category of Cultural Landscape on the 27 June 2011. It is the recognition by the international community of a territory that harmoniously combines human action with nature.

There are very few places where one comes across such orographical diversity in such a small area as in Mallorca. This fact resulted in the largest Balearic Island being visited and known for centuries by illustrious figures from all over the world. Indeed, at certain times, numerous artists have sought the source of their inspiration here. From the plain to the mountains, its territory was a sort of paradise, and despite recent pressures from tourism that have resulted in the loss of certain areas, especially along the coast, there are still an infinity of charming corners that give off the scent of past times. And although it is true that we can discover corners like this anywhere, it is in the magnificent Serra de Tramuntana —where the geography rebels against sudden changes— where we will find the scenery that best evokes these feelings.

In the Serra, gigantic ruins such as megalithic talayots, Roman remains, elements of the Islamic period, and the stunning presence of nature and of the rural world –so alive until recently and still hidden– invite one to enjoy a wide cultural experience in archaeology, botany, ornithology, anthropology… Whether we enjoy walking and climbing mountains to their tops or if we are enjoying the mobility of a vehicle. It is a delight to travel around the different environments of the immense mass that conceals extremely fertile valleys and nativity hamlets that lean out to sea and protect the rest of the island from the strongest winds. For this reason, in 2011 It was declared a UNESCO World Heritage Site in the category of Cultural Landscape.

The guide with facing map, with all the knowledge its authors would like to share, are offered to the reader with a great respect and love for this majestic environment. This guide should be a help in maximizing enjoyment of visits to this region, that, without a doubt will be several, as there is always something left to see or some memories that push one to return.

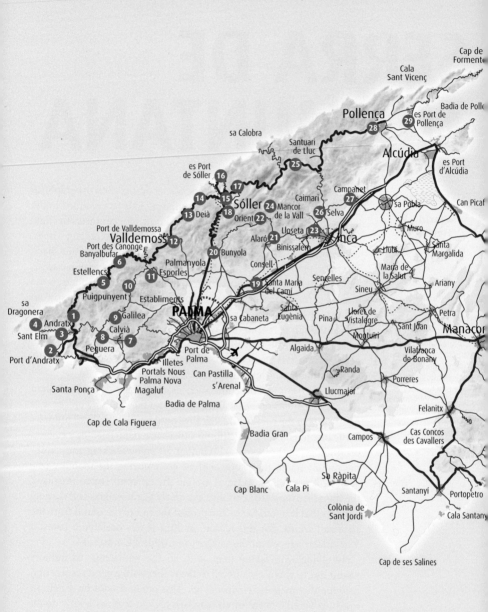

VILLAGES

d'Alcúdia
Cap Ferrutx
ia de
Pére
rtà Capdepera Cala Rajada
Son Servera Canyamel
t Llorenç Cala Bona
Cardassar Cala Millor
s'Illot
Portocristo
Cala Anguita
s de
orca
ocolom
'Or

Fornalutx

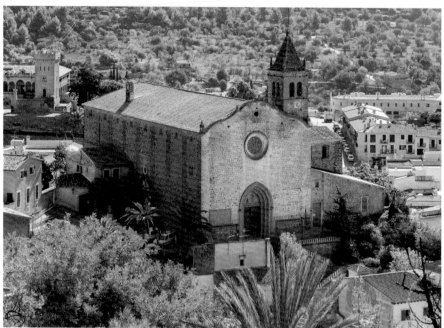

Church of Santa Maria at Andratx

Houses and tower of Son Mas, current town hall

PLACES OF INTEREST

SA DRAGONERA NATURAL PARK
P. 88

This islet watches over the coast of Andratx in the form of a sleeping dragon, inhabited by seagulls, lizards and Eleanor's falcons, with signposted routes on foot. Boats leave from Sant Elm that reach Sa Dragonera in 20 minutes.

❶ ANDRATX

This town, located in the west of Majorca, above the final foothills of the Serra de Tramuntana, maintains its distinction amongst the old quarters, Es Pantaleu, S'Almudaina and Es Pont d'Amunt, (dotted with whitewashed houses) and the more modern part that developed later and grew in recent years as a result of the notable demographic and urban growth in tourism. Its economy, that used to be based on agriculture and principally olive production, soap manufacture and overseas trade, has been transformed into being dependent on tourism, in continuous growth since the 1960's.

The view of the town must include the parish church of Santa Maria (18th century) and the two Latin crosses that delimit the town centre. One of these crosses, the **S'Abeurador cross**, is baroque and neogothic in style and is situated in the Plaça des Pou; the other, the **S'Ullastre cross**, situated in Carrer de Catalunya, is also baroque in style, with a small sundial carved into its shaft.

Upon leaving Andratx by the Estellencs road, one can see the houses of the estate and the tower of **Son Mas**, sentinels of a past of pirates and buccaneers who left their mark on the history of the town and its surroundings. Recently restored, it is the seat of the Andratx town hall.

From close to the church, we go towards the windmills of Sa Planeta, that observe the passage of time from the high part of the town. Two of them are still in a good state of preservation.

CELLARS FROM THE
SERRA DE TRAMUNTANA

SANTA CATARINA
Page **218-219**

Windmills of Sa Planeta

❷ PORT D'ANDRATX AND CAMP DE MAR

Port d'Andratx, which is very built up, is today the most important tourist enclave in the area. It was developed around the mouth of the Saluet torrent, from a small fishing village where fishermen moored their boats. Here one can visit the **church of Nostra Senyora del Carme**, that dates back from the beginning of the 20th century. For the best panoramic views of the area, one must go to Cap de sa Mola, that closes the port at the southeast. There, among luxury chalets, we will find the **tower of Sa Mola d'Andratx**, built in the 16th century

Port d'Andratx

on the ruins of an older one, that shows how even in remote times, there was already a pressing need to defend this coastline.

Going towards Andratx on the Morella road, which is ideal for going on foot or by bicycle, we can observe the houses of the farmstead of Son Orlandis and visit the hermitage of the same name, currently abandoned.

Further south, one comes across another urban centre that has grown to the rhythm of tourist development, but that still maintains in certain spots a great deal of placidity of days gone by. It is called **Camp de Mar**, from which it is easy to head on foot towards **Cap Andritxol**, with its circular plan tower from the 16th century. The area was declared a Nature Area of Special Interest (ANEI) owing to its enormous landscape value.

❸ S'ARRACÓ

The small village of S'Arracó, built around the church and encased between hills, is an example of the mix of old rural and modern tourism that is so frequent in the area. It emerged at the beginning of the 18th century from a chapel dedicated to Holy Christ, but the current church dates from 1742. Surrounded by olive groves, its image takes us back to a not too distant traditional agricultural past.

S'Arracó

Sant Elm. Sunset at Cala Conills and, against the light, Sa Dragonera

Facing Sa Dragonera is this estate of 75 hectares dedicated to environmental education, a beautiful spotwhere in 1810 a community of Trappist monks settled who had fled from the French Revolution to undertake a self-sufficient life, dedicated to prayer and working the land. It can only be reached by walking the 9 km from Sant Elm. At the top are the best views of Sa Dragonera.

❹ SANT ELM

Protected from the sea by the **Pantaleu** islet and facing west up to the island of **Sa Dragonera**, it was in former times a fishing centre. Transformed today into a summer holiday centre, one is reminded of the old times by the **Castell de Sant Elm**, with its defence tower that was built in 1302 and the chapel dedicated to the patron saint of sailors, recently restored buildings.

It is a good setting-off point for visiting various places of interest. One of these visits is on the island of Sa Dragonera, on a boat that leaves regularly form the small harbour of Sant Elm. Anothr classic trip is to the state of **La Trapa** (see route on foot 1, on pages 142-144). Another walk leads us from Sant Elm to the tower of Cala en Basset (16th century), with a spectacular panoramic view. From the tower, we can also drop down to the cove of the same name. Also starting off from Sant Elm is a road that takes one to Cala d'Egos.

View of Sant Elm, with the islet of Es Pantaleu and Sa Dragonera

⑤ ESTELLENCS

At the foot of Puig de Galatzó, this small village sits on the same slope of the mountain. It has steeply sloped evocative cobbled streets that are narrow and labyrinthine and bear witness to their adaptation to the terrain and the fear of pirate attacks of the 15th to the 18th centuries. Apart from strolling through the village, it is worth visiting the small cove located on the coast at the foot of the town centre, namely, **Port d'Estellencs**.

The walk starts at the **church of Sant Joan Baptista**. Standing out on the façade is one-piece portal lintel with a triangular pediment that shows a pyramid with a sphere in each corner. On the left of the façade and encased in the church is the quadrangular bell tower that was also a defence tower. In a side street of Carrer de la Síquia, at the end of a small garden enclosure, we can see the ruins of an unfinished church of the 19th century. Let us continue our visit with the **Tem Alemany tower**, located in Plaça des Triquet. It dates, apparently, from the 16th century and it was one of the three defence towers of the village of Estellencs together with the church and another that has disappeared. At the entrance of the village there is the old **public washhouse**. Water comes from the Forat d'Amunt spring that, having passed through the washhouse, is distributed along the terraces by means of the irrigation channel of the Regants des Forat d'Amunt.

CELLARS FROM THE
SERRA DE TRAMUNTANA
TOMEU ISERN
Page **218-219**

Panorama of Estellencs with the Puig de Galatzó in the background

**CHEESE
AND WINE FAIR**
Every May Estellencs holds this fair dedicated to the cheeses and wines of Mallorca, with the presence of the best wine cellars of the island and traditional cheese producers, such as those made with the milk of the Mallorca *red sheep*.

Street in Estellencs

Terraces at Banyalbufar

Banyalbufar

CELLARS FROM THE
SERRA DE TRAMUNTANA

CA'N PICÓ
SON VIVES
COOPERATIVA
DE SA MALVASIA
Page 218-219

❻ BANYALBUFAR

It has a mountainous and rugged geography, with sheer coastal cliffs that reach a maximum height of 934 metres at La Mola de Planícia. In Arabic, *Bahaia al-bujar* means "building close to the sea" and the inheritance from the era of Islamic domination includes terraces, reservoirs, irrigation channels, canals and bridges; this irrigation system corresponds to the so called *ma'jil*, which is Arabic in origin.

The parish church of **Nativitat de Santa Maria**, in front of Plaça de la Vila, contains the organ that came from the Sant Domingo Covent in Palma. The organ, brought to Banyalbufar in 1847, is attributed to the Dominican Vicenç Pizà. The large altarpiece dates from 1787; it is classicist in style and is the work of Mateu Colom. It is presided over by a painting that represents the birth of the Virgin.

La Baronia, a beautiful example of 16th century architecture, is the most important civic building in Banyalbufar. It was the centre of feudal life in another era, with a baronial jurisdiction that covered practically the entire valley. The façade is located on the side of the road, opposite the side of the church and most surprising is the beautiful patio that one enters via a large low arch (17th century) that at the time served as a bridge between the various outbuildings of the main house and the tower. A part of the building was converted into a hotel in 1952.

The area of **Es Penyal** is situated further up from the town centre. One walks up to it via the stepped Carrer de s'Amargura which is next to the façade of the church; one turns into Carrer del Penyal; going up the steps one passes through Can Ros and El Pastador. The stepped ground appears to be paved with reddish flagstones. A left turn leaves us close to a viewpoint over the village and the sea. A right turn allows us to continue on the last stretch of the ascent, and reach group houses of Es Penyal. At the end of the quarter, a small road takes us up to the nearby terraces and to the Síquia de Baix (irrigation channel).

Interior patio of Sa Baronia

Calvià

⑦ CALVIÀ

In the church square there is a **historical/geographical mural** of the municipality. It is a panel of polychrome tiles that was made in 1986 by the Escola Taller de Belles Arts de Calvià. It represents a tree with details of the history of Mallorca and with particular references to the history of the municipality. Carrying on, we reach the series of buildings made up of the parish parish **church of Sant Joan Baptista** and the **Rectory**. The parish church was built between 1867 and 1896. It is in historicist style, where neo-Romanesque and neo-Gothic elements are combined. We find at Carrer Major 85, Can Verger that rises at the bottom of an open space that was used as a garden and which today houses the Calvià Public Library. On the way out of the town, there is **La Capelleta**; a small 15th century oratory dedicated to the Mare de Déu dels Dolors that also gives its name to the street. In front, there is a boundary cross that was rebuilt in a modern style in Santanyí stone. As interesting examples of the town's architecture, we will concentrate on the houses of **Cal Metge Vell**, on the other side of the tarmac, on whose higher part rises a neo-Arabic turret. We also concentrate on the houses of **Can Ros**, at the end of the road of the same name, where there is an old olive-oil mill. If we return to the square, we find in Carrer Major, at the junction with Carrer de Can Vic, the old cistern, **l'aljub Vell**, one of the most important elements, together with the **Nou** and **de Dalt** cisterns, in the water supply to Calvià. **Es Pontet** is one of the oldest houses in the town, with its northern façade located in Carrer del Pontet and its western one, that can be considered its main one, rising above an avenue. An example of traditional rural architecture are the houses of the *possessió* (a name given to an estate or property in Majorca that is often repeated in this guide) **Mofarès** —the origin of which is an old Muslim farm called *Mofarig* that today is used for rural tourism— at the end of the cart track that comes out onto the Calvià to Capdellà road.

The **Castellet mill** is an old flour windmill, situated 230 metres high on a hill north of the town called El Castellet.

ORNITHOLOGICAL ROUTES
In the pine groves, holm-oak woods, riverside woods, coast and mountains of Calvià there are many birds, and for bird lovers a website has been created with suggestions for bird-spotting routes to see them and describes the most typical species.
www.birdingcalvia.com

Historical-geographical mural of the Calvià municipal area

Es Capdellà;
a corner of Can Pagès

⑧ ES CAPDELLÀ

Leaving Calvià and heading towards the interior of the western area, one reaches this small rural village that has Puig de Galatzó as a background. It still relies on its agricultural activities and the environment is authentically tranquil. In the centre of the village we can visit the church, modern and rebuilt In the second half of the 20th century, the **Pou Nou** (new well) and, a little further on, the **Capdellà mill**. If we continue to the Peguera road, we find the **Son Vic Vell** *possessió*. Returning to the village and taking the road to Galilea, prior to crossing the Na Corba torrent, the **Galatzó houses** road starts. The property has recently been bought by the Calvià Town Council and is the most legendary estate in the area. Here, the Comte Mal myth started that tells of the second count of Formiguera who was condemned to roam around the world on a fire-horse. Over the door of the chapel one can see the noble coat of arms from 1688 and an inscription with the count's name.

Interior of the parish church of La Immaculada Concepció, in Galilea

⑨ GALILEA

This village in the municipal district of Puigpunyent is between Es Capdellà and Puigpunyent. It is perched on a hill, just a short distance from the Puig de Galatzó. It is worth climbing to admire the clocks in the church square, and the excellent panorama of the bay of Palma and the Pla region. It is a good viewpoint and, if there are no strong winds, which often sweep the village, you can sit down for a while on the terrace of the Bar Parroquial (restaurant Ca n'Andreu) or the Sa Plaça bar. We can visit the **parish church** devoted to the Immaculate and the **Pou des Rafal** in the street of the same name, and, heading for that of La Mola, one can see a *casa de neu* (snow storage house) and the two mills of **Can Soler** and **d'en Martí** in the high part.

⑩ PUIGPUNYENT

CELLARS FROM THE
SERRA DE TRAMUNTANA

SON PUIG
Page **218-219**

Four kilometres further on and sharing the same municipality as Galilea, Puigpunyent receives us with a welcome of crops, fruit trees and woods. The **Vila** quarter is the first one sees, with its 18th century **church of Assumpció de Nostra Senyora**, rebuilt over a 13th century church. Around it, one can see old houses and, if one descends towards the Sa Riera torrent, one can see, on top of a hill, the house of the estate of **Son Net** that have been converted into a hotel. On the other side of the torrent, along the street called Sa Travessia, there is the **Serral** quarter where one can see an old covered well, the **Pou Nou**, very close to the Town Hall and the Casa de Cultura. From here it is worth walking along Carrer Major up to the junction with the Trast street and then returning along the Serral street up to the set off point.

Church of Puigpunyent

⑪ ESPORLES

This village, that grew on the banks of the Sant Pere torrent and parallel to the road that gives it access to Palma, has drunk water and gained wealth from the torrent. It offers beautiful walks through its well-minded streets. If we start in the **Sa Vileta** quarter, one of the oldest in the village, at the northernmost end of the avenue we will see the **church of Sant Pere** that is neogothic with three 17th century altarpieces in its interior. Next to it is the façade of the **Rectoria** that has a round arched portal and a **water trough** that together make up a rural image of great beauty. Without leaving this area, a sculpture by Remigia Caubet, *La filadora* (the spinner) catches one's attention. This is located in front of the Town Hall and bears witness to the importance in the mid-19th century of the textile industry in the village and especially the manufacture of woollen blankets. One is also reminded of this by the **chapel of Sant Crist de la Pols**, patron of the weaving trade, which was in the landscaped area in front of the Passeig del Rei. A visit is not complete without a stroll through the narrow streets of **Vila Vella**.

Once on the outskirts at a little over two kilometres in a westerly direction of the Verger road and after the **Son Tries recreation area** and just before the houses of the estate of Son Ferrà, one goes through a metal gate where a small path starts that leads, on foot, to the **hermitage of Maristel·la**. This is one of the most attractive places in the municipality where there is as good view over all the valley. From here, one can continue the ascent, a more difficult excursion, to **Fita des Ram** (833 m) that widens the view even more to the Andratx valley and the coast.

PLACES OF INTEREST

POSSESSIÓ **LA GRANJA**
P. 99

A stately home in the middle of a leafy landscape, the visit to which represents a journey in time back to rural Mallorca. They have farm animals, traditional tools and furniture. In their carefully kept gardens grows a venerable millenary yew tree.
www.lagranja.net

CELLARS FROM THE SERRA DE TRAMUNTANA
ES VERGER SON VICH DE SUPERNA
Page **218-219**

Carrer des Balladors

The Rectory

Carrer de Darrera sa Paret

⑫ VALLDEMOSSA

The town of Valldemossa presents two very outstanding centres of attraction. The first is the monastic complex of **La Cartoixa** and the second is the narrow and often winding set of streets that surround the parish church.

Even though La Cartoixa merits a separate chapter (see pages 91-94), we will take a glance here and gaze out from the exterior of **Palau del Rei Sanç** and **Cartoixa Vella,** close to the square dedicated to Rubén Dario (formerly Pati des Brollador), with its pointed arched portal that was formerly the entrance and above which a relief of Sant Bru calls for our attention. Further south, we contemplate the beautiful view afforded by the **Miranda dels Lledoners,** at the foot of the Hostes tower that dates from 1555.

From Ramon Llull square we will advance towards the oldest part of the town via Carrer de Uetam, with La Cartoixa orchard on our right. On Carrer de la Constitució we have on our left the former **Town Hall** building, known locally as **El Porxo**. It has a sundial and the year 1605 inscribed on it. Continuing downwards on the slight slope, we reach Santa Catalina Tomàs square, in which we find the parish **church of Sant Bartomeu,** already documented in the 13th century. Its interior contains an important baroque altarpiece dating from 1720 that preserves an image of the Assumption that dates from the first half of the 16th century. The baptismal font dates from the end of the 17th century and the Sacrarium chapel is dedicated to Santa Catalina Tomàs. Next to the side door of the church there is the **Rectory,** one of the many interesting buildings in the town. A few metres away, Nr. 5 is the house where **Santa Catalina Tomàs** was born, converted into a chapel, with an image of the Valldemossa saint.

Our suggestion is to continue with a route in the old quarter of the town through its

LA TRINITAT

At km 69.9 of the road from Valldemossa to Deià, opposite the Can Costa restaurant, the path begins that leads to this century-old hermitag, an idyllic spot with a picnic area in the shade. There have been hermits in the area since the 13th century, capable —according to the fishermen— of stopping a tornado with the sign of the cross.

Valldemossa; parish church

PLACES OF INTEREST

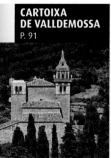

CARTOIXA DE VALLDEMOSSA
P. 91

The Polish composer Frédéric Chopin and the French writer George Sand stayed in the Cartoixa de Valldemossa, in the 19th century turned into a residence for the wealthy and foreigners.

narrow streets, seeing the enchanting **Carrer de la Rectoria**, that of Pare Castanyeda, traditionally known by the name of Carrer de la Amargura, the **Baix boundary cross** and the **Beata fountain** with its images of Sant Antoni and Santa Catalina Tomàs, that remind one of her miracles and also varied houses with painted roofs. Also interesting are: the **Plaça Pública** —that has a classic colonnade with four Moorish segmental arches that takes in the old market and the inn of the Trinitat hermits—, **Can Salvà**, with a round arched portal crowned with a coat of arms in Carrer de la Rosa 35. Very close by there is **Cal Sabater Coix**, with an arched portal that contains an anagram of Christ; **Son Ronqueto** at 35 Carrer del Rei Sanç that has two reliefs in the form of a head with a gorget and finally, the **cross of L'Abeurador**, with interesting miniature reliefs. The wash house and the drinking trough are close by and if all the above are not enough, we can cross the road and visit the **houses of Son Gual** that have a spectacular defence tower.

The old quarter of the town

Valldemossa

⑬ DEIÀ

A small mountain village with a rugged geography, it gives protection to Cala de Deià and reaches a maximum height of 1,062 metres at Puig des Teix, whose northern slopes rise up dizzily over the village and its surrounding areas. According to Corominas, the etymology of Deià comes from the Arabic *daia*, meaning hamlet. Over time, its charm has attracted well-known artists from all over the world —writers, painters...— who installed themselves in Deià. The charm of **Llucalcari** and some emblematic *possessions*, such as **Son Marroig**, with **Sa Foradada**, and **Ca l'Abat**, complete this "nativity village" as it was called by Santiago Rusiñol.

The road that leads from Valldemossa becomes the main street of Deià, the centre of the town's economic and social life. At the entrance of the town centre, we come to the Fresca fountain, with the wash house and a paved road that goes up to the **Racó quarter.** On the other side, an alley allows us to make a tour of the **Clot quarter** and its cobbled streets. Until recently it was the Archaeological Museum of Deià, which in 2017 remained closed. Founded in 1962 by the North American archaeologist William Waldren, it contains an exhibition of the prehistoric Balearics, in particular the excavations of the municipalities of Sóller, Deià and Valldemossa. Outstanding is the copy of the Dama de Son Matge, a small statue representing the outline of a woman and some skeletons of *Myotragus balearicus*. Further down we reach the mountain refuge called Can Boi, whichh contains an Interesting oil factory. At the beginning of the Ribassos path, which reaches the Cala de Deià, is the narrow path of the **Molí fountain** and, a little lower down, **some small wash houses**.

Continuing through the district along the road, on the right we come to the houses of **Can Fussimany**, with a very interesting outer portal, from 1618, which follows the style known as rustic Manierist. It has been a hotel complex called La Residència since 1984 and occupies two old large houses, **Son Canals** and **Son Moragues**, and still conserves the defence tower and olive mill.

On the other side of the road, towards the town centre, we come to **Can Vallés**, a country house in regionalist style ordered to be built by Antoni Vives, secretary of Archduke Lluís Salvador. Close

! PLACES OF INTEREST

POSSESSIÓ **SON MARROIG**
P. 103

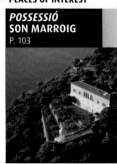

Impressive *possessió* acquired in 1870 by the Archduke Ludwig Salvator of Austria, who reformed the house and had a neoclassical shrine built in the garden, from where one can see the point of Sa Foradada, and on clear days, Sa Dragonera.

INTERNATIONAL FESTIVAL OF DEIÀ
Since 1978, between May and September, this festival dedicated mainly to chamber music has been held, one of the most prestigious in Mallorca. The concerts are held on large stages such as Son Marroig, Miramar or the church of Deià.
www.dimf.com

Image of the village of Deià

A beautiful corner of the village

by, in Carrer del Porxo, stands the town hall; it occupies the site of an old building dated 1584 whichh housed the meetings of the municipal council of Deià, then recently separated from Valldemossa. Very close by, the Sant Joan fountain, covered by a chapel, contains a series of ceramic floor tiles that depict the child Baptist.

From the fountain, we climb to the **Des Puig quarter**. The **Stations of the Cross** that surrounds the streets of Des Puig is quite outstanding, made up of small quadrangular chapels that contain the ceramic floor tiles of the corresponding station. At the top of Des Puig stands the **church of San Joan Baptista**; it has a single rectangular nave, with barrel vaulting ceiling and side chapels. And in front of the church is the **cemetery**, where the remains lay of artists such as the painters Gelabert, Leman and Ribes, the writer Robert Graves or the Mallorcan playwright Joan Mas. In the setting of the Plaça de l'Església we come to **Can Lau des Puig**, one of the oldest houses In the town. The **Posada des Molí** is a house that conserves painted roof tiles.

THE DEIÀ OF ROBERT GRAVES

Robert Graves, British poet, novelist and scholar, settled in Deià in 1929 with his partner, the North American poet Laura Riding. He produced the greater part of his work in Deià: several editions of poems and numerous books in prose, among then *I Claudius* and the essay *The White Goddess*. The writer also remains linked to the cove of Llucalcari, where he wrote his *Twenty-one Love Poems*.

The cemetery of Deià

⑭ LLUCALCARI

Fourteen houses grouped together and eight more scattered around make up this small village. It comes under the Deià municipality and in 1991 there were 10 registered inhabitants who are called *carrerencs*, as it also called **Es Carrer**. Etymologically, Llucalcari can be interpreted as a word composed of the Latin derivative *lluc* (wood) and the Arabic *qari* (farmsteads). The origin could also come from the first Arabic particle *luk* that gives us *lloc* with the meaning of hamlet —an inhabited place.

Apart from the **chapel of Mare de Déu dels Desemparats** and Can Junyer, currently closed, which should be the headquarters of the Fundació Junyer, three houses are preserved with attached defence towers: **Can Apol·loni**, the best preserved, that is currently the Hotel Costa d'Or, **Casa d'Amunt**, the tallest, and **Can Simó**, that also has a square ground plan tower.

Llucalcari. In the background, the Punta de Sa Pedrissa, the entrance to Cala de Deià

⑮ SÓLLER

The valley of Sóller, rich in history and surrounded by an amphi-theatre of mountains, affords a suggestive and enriching visit. We shall start in Sóller at the **parish church of Sant Bartomeu**. The church was built between 1688 and 1811, with a baroque outline but also with certain traditional gothic elements. The main façade, built between 1904 and 1947, was designed by Joan Rubió i Bellver, a disciple of Gaudí, and followed a modernist style. The rustic treatment of the calcareous stone contributes to its aesthetic goal. In the area surrounding the building we can see remains of medi-eval arcades and windows and the walled formation from the 16th century city walls.

We continue along the **Banc de Sóller**, situated in the church square and which dates from 1911, and which features the projected double gallery, the semi-circular arcade and the wrought iron of the windows. It was also built in Modernist style by the same architect of the façade of the neighbouring church, with which it combines stylistically. We continue along Carrer de Sa Lluna, where we notice the **Posada de Can Prohom**, a tradi-tional ancestral home of three floors, **Casa de la Lluna**, of medieval origin and with a curious relief of the moon on the front door which gives the building and the street their name, and **Can Prunera**, another Modernist house from 1911 —currently the home of the **Museu Modernista**— which has a permanent col-lection of contemporary art and a library specialising in art where they display books illustrated by the painter Joan Miró, closely linked to the island for a large part of his life. Outstanding are the stained-glass windows, the mural paintings in polychrome relief, the furnishing and other elements such as the inner stairway or the main façade. Since it was opened as a museum in 2009, Can Prunera has been a cultural reference point in the valley of Sóller.

In the environs, we discover the **chapel of Mare de Déu de la Victoria**, the **Posada de Montcaire**, from

Museu Modernista Can Prunera

Tren de Sóller bridge, in the background the Son Torrella range

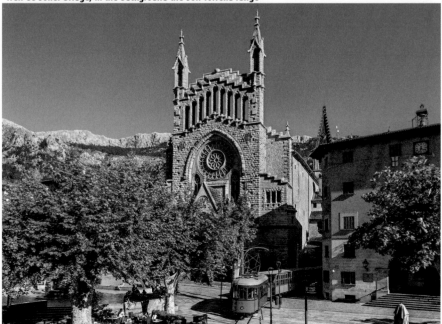

The Plaça de la Constitució

the 18th century, and the **Posada de Bàlitx** from the 17th century. **Can Mo**, a building that houses the Casal de la Cultura, has been fitted out as an exhibition hall, a library and an ethnological museum.

The **Gran Via** has been an important solleric suburban avenue from the early 20th century. It was born out of the great commercial and economic boom of the final years of the 19th century. Here one can see interesting houses, many of which are prime examples of modernism. Outstanding are the **Rectoria**, from 1896; **Can Magraner**, a modernist house attributed to Joan Rubió (with a balcony in which

Botanical garden, with the Puig Major in the background

the surname Magraner is engraved); **Can Dulce**, dedicated to a cultural centre and **Can Cremat**, dating from 1922, with an outstanding portico made up of six compound capital columns.

The **Convent de Sóller** was founded in 1458 on land situated in the Camí Vell de Ciutat. The new convent, taking its place, was built in the 18th century. The chapel contains the Christ de Sóller, that sweated blood when the bandit Benet Esteve refused to convert in the 16th century. The cloister was completed in 1798. It has a square ground plan with seven segmental arches on each side, supported by Ionic style columns.

The **Museu Balear de Ciències Naturals** is located in a big house that dates from the early 20th century, namely, the Cases des Camp d'en Prohom. It contains, most importantly, the micro-fossil collections of the geologist Guillem Colom i Casasnovas (1900-1993), a native of the town, and a library specializing in micropalaeontology. On the ground floor of the building one can currently visit the "Història de las Ciències Naturals a las illes Balears" hall. On the upper floor, a part of the Joan Bauçà palaeontology collection, recently donated to the museum, is on exhibition.

On the lands that surround the house (approx. 10,000 m^2) one finds the **Jardí Botànic de Sóller**, the most complete and important on the island, with plots of Balearic and Canary Island flora.

On the outskirts, along Camí Vell de Fornalutx, we come across the hamlet of **Binibassí**. The main houses rise in front of the proud gardens that contain cypresses, date palms, oleanders and ivy, amongst other species. There is a defence tower with a square ground plan that is five stories high. It dates back from the 16th century. The projection of the patio contains painted tiles; there is also a preserved oil press that dates from the 18th century and a private chapel or oratory, with an altarpiece of 1753. The houses were restored in 1871. Close to the main house, to the west, there is a second house called **Can Ballester**; even further west, there continues the old road that leads to Sóller.

To the northeast of the main houses, along Camí Vell de Fornalutx there is the **Molí de l'Hort**, a water-powered flour mill; it has an original circular section tower. It appears to have been built in the 15th or 16th century and was in use until the 19th century.

Paintings by Anna David illustrate the offer of Sa Fàbrica de Gelats

Port de Sóller

⑯ PORT DE SÓLLER

The picturesque tram that links the town of Sóller to its harbour is the ideal means to visit it. Located in a shelter of the bay between **Cap Gros** in the west and the **Picada tower** that protects it from the north, Port de Sóller possesses an old fishing quarter, that of **Santa Catalina**, that has a chapel of the same name. It faces the **Creu des Port** and the nearby **Sa Miranda**, that is a fantastic viewpoint of the bay.

Walking down the steps of Carrer de Santa Apol·lònia, one arrives at the chapel of **Sant Ramon de Penyafort** that boasts the legend that claims that from a stone close to this building, the saint set off on a crossing from Majorca to Barcelona on his cape, with his walking stick as his mast. Made angry by the criticism directed towards King Jaume I by the saint, the king prohibited any boat to take the saint on board. All this happened around 1232.

Returning back, we visit the new parish church of Ramon de Penyafort and crossing the bridge of the Sa Figuera torrent, we find steps that lead to the ***Possessió* des Port**, whose houses, with a defence tower and a beautiful paved patio, have been transformed into a hotel.

The nets of the fishing boats are today still kept on the jetty and, very close, a cluster of pleasure boats indicates that this is also an important tourist harbour. A long beach of fine sand welcomes bathers and in its environs, various services make summer holidaying a totally pleasant experience.

The walk to **Punta des Cap Gros**, is highly recommended. Here one can see the oldest lighthouse in Mallorca, in the words of Archduke Ludwig Salvator; close by, there is today a mountain refuge, the **Muleta** refuge. On the other side of the bay, we can go to the place called **Es Bufador**, in which one finds the **Punta de la Creu lighthouse**; a further walk takes us to **Torre Picada**, mentioned at the start, that is one of the biggest defence towers on the island, built in the 17th century. If one wishes to return to Sóller on foot, we would recommend taking **Camí de sa Figuera**, a small road with a very picturesque route, and a series of well-signposted public paths for pedestrians and walkers, such as that of Binidorm or the Coll d'en Borrassà.

TRAIN AND TROLLEY

The train of Sóller is a wooden narrow gauge railway line that has linked Palma with Sóller since 1912, and since 1913 a trolley has connected Sóller with Port de Sóller. A comfortable journey in time and space with good frequency of trains. www.trendesoller.com

⑰ FORNALUTX

From the Torrent de la Vall de Sóller to the top, this village climbs in the direction of the hillsides of Puig Major and preserves, virtually intact, a valuable architectural and landscape heritage. A total of twenty- eight houses show painted tiles on their eaves, which is a very common tradition in the valley and which is probably Islamic in origin. Indeed, the popular local name of these tiles is *teules de moro*. One of these houses is known by the name of **Es Puador**; also remarkable are the houses of **Can Estades**, the **Posada de Bàlitx** (one of the most characteristic and oldest big houses in the village), **Can Bisbal** (second oldest), the **Casa d'Amunt** (medieval in origin, that housed the Posada de Montcaire until 1881) and **Can Xandre**, in the church square.

The village of Fornalutx

The present parish church, situated on the old gothic church, was started in 1613 and finished at the end of the 17th century. The Town Hall is located in an old 16th-century house, **Can Arbona**, that preserves a tall and slender defence tower. Very close by (Carrer de la Font, 8) stands **Can Xoroi**, a public building that shows the oil press and an exhibition of painted tiles. Further down, there is the public wash house, known as **Es Raig**. This has recently been restored and has a tiled roof.

The public wash house of Fornalutx is named Es Raig

⑱ BINIARAIX

This is a hamlet that was born next to the torrent of Biniaraix and is very close to Sóller. It is notable for its paved and narrow streets that are dotted with orange trees. Its water is supplied by the Biniaraix spring that fills the beautiful washhouse. In addition to the 17th-century church, there are old houses such as **Cas Don** and others, with painted tiles on their projections. The **Biniaraix ravine** that reaches the Ofre estate is an exceptional element of the Camí Vell from Sóller to Lluc, with a difference in height of more than 600 m along its length of some three kilometres.

A Biniaraix street

⑲ SANTA MARIA DEL CAMÍ

This is a municipality in the Raiguer region that presents two very different parts. The areas of the south are flat with almond trees and vines and are the backdrop to the Puig de Son Seguí. The areas of the north reach the foothills of the Serra de Tramuntana, surrounded by enchanting places, like the **Coanegra valley**.

In the town centre there are two outstanding quarters: **Els Hostals** and **La Vila**. In the former, people would stay there in times gone by when they travelled on the roads that link the mountains with the plains and those who travelled on the Palma to Inca road. Preserved there is an ancient public well, **Sa Sínia**, that originates from the prehistoric era and continued in use during the Islamic domination and subsequent eras. Also in this area are the church, the convent, the cloister of the Mínims (**Can Conrado**) and, in front of the convent, the colonnades of the old boarding houses. A little further, on the other side of the train station, we can see the **Son Güia mill**. In **La Vila** we find the **Casa de la Vila** with its gothic altarpiece of Santa Maria del Camí (14th century) and the **parish church** from the 18th century, whose bell tower displays characteristic tiles.

If we go up to the town via the magnificent Coanegra road (see itinerary 8 on page 171), we have the opportunity to see the houses of Son Torrella, a beautiful estate of medieval origin.

CELLARS FROM THE
SERRA DE TRAMUNTANA

**JAUME DE PUNTIRÓ
MACIÀ BATLE
RAMANYÀ
SEBASTIÀ PASTOR
ANGEL
7103 PETIT CELLER**
Page **218-219**

Santa Maria del Camí

SUNDAY MARKET

Santa Maria holds its weekly market on Sundays, with stalls selling clothes, ceramics, basketwork, handicrafts, fruit and vegetables, and a wide variety of organic products. You should get up early to wander around at your leisure and have breakfast in a bar in the square.

PLACES OF INTEREST

RAIXA AND ALFÀBIA
P. 94 and 97

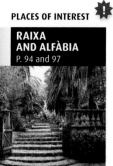

The district of Bunyola houses two stately *possessions* fundamentally linked to the history of Mallorca, Raixa and Alfàbia, which can be visited.

⓴ BUNYOLA

Protected by the Serra de Alfabia, the town stretches out from the Sóller train station. Sunny and surrounded by woods such as **Sa Comuna**, the town centre offers one a relaxed visit with stop-offs at various points of interest. Amongst these we mention **Sa Creu**, built of marès stone and on the way to the square we find **Can Villa-longa**. This is a house attached completely to the present Town Hall building and was acquired in 1853 by Guillem Villalonga, grandfather of the writer Llorenç Villalonga. We also mention the **parish church of Sant Mateu**, already linked to the papal bull of Innocent IV in 1248. The present church, perhaps the third religious building on the same site, dates from between 1756 and 1786 and is baroque in style. Following on the Carrer Major, we find what remains of the **houses of Son Garcies**, that were the most important in Bunyola. The exterior portal still exists, with its segmental arch that leads to a beamed vestibule and an irregular inner patio. The **Rectoria**, located in the Rector Marroig square, was formerly the seat of the local Universitat, where the royal oil mill was once installed, also called Tafona del Delme. To the right of the Rectory there is a 17th century house of traditional architecture called **Can Bava**. It has three stories, an arched portal and a porch with a sliding door, as well as a decorated façade where one can still see traces of graffti.

The high part of Bunyola is made up of the **Barracar quarter**, that borders on the Carrer Orient, where we find old and beautiful stepped passageways such as L'Aigua, La Lluna and others.

Parish church of Sant Mateu

Puig d'Alaró and Puig d'Alcadena

Plaça de la Vila, Alaró

CELLARS FROM THE
SERRA DE TRAMUNTANA

**CASTELL MIQUEL
VINYES D'ALARÓ**
Page **218-219**

㉑ ALARÓ

This forms part of the Raiguer region and is situated at the southern heel of the Serra de Tramuntana. Puig de sa Font Seca reaches a maximum height of 836m, followed by Puig d'Alaró at 825m, on which is located **the castle of Alaró**. The etymology of Alaró comes from the Arab *al'-run* which means "Roman, Byzantine or Christian", and refers to the castle of Alaró.

Around the square we find a large part of the town's architectural heritage: the **parish church of Sant Bartomeu**, an old gothic church of which only the bell tower remains. It was replaced by the present baroque church that was started in 1626 and finished in 1785. Its interior was painted by the Italian painter, A.Soldati. The bronze sculpture entitled *Retorn al bon camí* (Return to the good path) is located opposite the church, on the other side of the square, and is an original by the Alaró sculptor, Llorenç Rosselló. The **Creu d'en Coix**, located on the left side of the church, dates from the 16th century and is gothic in style. The **Town Hall**, a stone building built in 1941, has an inner patio in which there are the remains of some arches and the town's coat of arms from 1681. There is also the **Posada de Can Xalet** dating from the 18th century that is also known by the name of Can Barrantina. It is presently occupied by the Can Punta restaurant. In a nearby street there are the **houses of Son Mallol** that are three stories high; there is a lanced round arched portal. The building is 18th century and contains a preserved oil press that was the last one in use in Alaró. In **Celler de s'Olivaret**, a nearby building of the 17th and 18th centuries, there are *botes congrenyades* (butts with wooden hoops) from the same period that are still used for storing wine.

From the Plaça de la Vila one needs to head northwest to reach **los Damunt**, a typical and old quarter that was the original centre of Alaró. In the centre, the square, with a small chapel dedicated to the defenders of the castle of Alaró, Cabrit and Bassa, has a public cistern that collects water from Ses Artigues fountain. **La Bastida** is one of the most representative large houses of the town. From here we can go to the small **quarter of Es Pujol**, where there is a good view of the **Vila d'Avall** and the houses of the estates of **Son Borràs**

EL RAIGUER

The capital of this large inland county is Inca, known for its age-old and prosperous leather industry. It comprises a trickle of villages where tradition and good food rule, since it is the land of farmers and *cellers*, old wine cellars transformed into restaurants that preserve the most authentic Mallorca gastronomy.

and **Son Bieló**. The latter contains ruins of an Islamic mill and a chapel. **Son Vidal** is also an old 17th-century building.

In Ponterró, to the northeast of the town, there are the house of **Son Tugores**, with a 17th-century portal, **Can Jaumico**, a house with modernist elements and the old **Posada de Bànyols** from the 18th and 19th centuries. On the front of the house there is a stone cross set to the wall, **Sa Creu**, and towards the outskirts there are **the Ponterró wash house** and the houses of the estate of **Son Mas**.

What is left to see is the **Rectoria**, the old **Posada of Son Guitard**, an 18th-century building, and what is left of the first electricity power station of Majorca, the so called **Torre des Llum** (light tower). The most outstanding buildings on the outskirts of Alaró are also worth visiting. **Son Fortesa**, a 16th-century building, rises in front of an avenue filled with hackberries, plane trees and cypresses. It is a two-story building with an external lanced round arch and keystone portal. The Safortesa coat of arms (three fleur-de-lis) crowns the portal. **Bànyols** was an Islamic farmstead, from which its place name probably derives, where a mosque was documented up to the 14th century.

From the town a road starts that can be travelled by car until Pla des Pouet; it reaches the **castle of Alaró**, an imposing fortification that was already documented in the Islamic era. It is situated strategically over the crags. The last section, which is paved, leaves us in front of the entrance door that has a rounded arch. Climbing some steps one gains access to the keep. Continuing along the road, we reach a viewpoint from which one can gaze at the mountains and further on we come across **the inn and the chapel of Mare de Déu del Refugi**, declared a cultural heritage interest site in 1985.

The castle of Alaró

㉒ ORIENT

This is a hamlet of stepped streets climb up to the **church of Sant Jordi**. The church was probably built over an ancient chapel of the 13th century. A few old houses, most of which have been restored for use as second homes, give this place its particular character. At the lower part of the village we find the **washhouse** and the **Creu dels Llavadosos**, made of *marès* stone. On the outskirts, the houses of the estate of **Son Terrassa** and those of **Cals Reis** are notable. They have an outer portal that leads directly to the patio on whose right side there is an oil mill with a portal dated 1640.

㉓ LLOSETA

This is a village of feudal origin, also bordering between the Serra and the Raiguer and receiving its water from the Almadrà torrent. As for its architectural heritage, notable are, in the town centre, the **Palau d'Aiamans**, dating from the 18th and 20th centuries, surrounded by gardens and declared a cultural heritage interest site by the Govern de les Illes Balears; attached to the palace is the **parish church**, a neoclassical building from the mid-18th century in which one can see a Romanesque carving of the Mare de Déu de Lloseta and to the right, a chapel containing the crypt of the counts of Aiamans. The **Plaça d'Espanya** is also notable. As with many other towns, one can see the differences between the high part, with a traditional structure and steep streets, and the low part, with a more modern structure. Leaving by the Alaró road, we come across the **Cocó chapel** and, via the Almadrà road, the houses of **Des Filcomís** and high on the right, those of **S'Estorell**.

TOSSALS VERDS REFUGE

In the Clot d'Almadrà in Lloseta a three-hour walk begins to the Tossals Verds refuge, which forms part of the long-distance path, the *Ruta de la Pedra en Sec*, with some wonderful views. It is well worth eating and sleeping in the refuge, booking in advance. www.conselldemallorca.net

㉔ MANCOR DE LA VALL

Hiking enthusiasts appreciate this village that is situated at the foot of the Puig de Massanella (1,349m). We can start the visit to the town centre from the neoclassical **church of Sant Joan Baptista** that has a lintelled portal crowned by a triangular gable on the façade and an interior of only one nave and side chapels.

Also notable are various houses, such as **Son Morro**, in Carrer Salvador Beltran, that has a 17th-century oil press that was in use until 1930, and **Son Collell**, at 25, Carrer Bartomeu Reus, with its curious patio in which there is the entrance door to the bakery. Also, there is **Turixant**, at the end of the same street, that today has been turned into a restaurant.

The **Manacor fountain**, already documented in the year 1232, is a *qanat* from the Islamic era. The fountain complex, with its troughs and wash house, was restored in 1991.

We can now go, in the surrounding area, to the **chapel of Santa Llúcia** and to the **Biniarroi** farmstead or, by following the Caimari road, to the houses of the estate of **Massanella**.

FAIR OF THE ESCLATA-SANG (BLOODY MILK CAP)

In November, Mancor holds this fair of the bloody milk cap, in which collectors and craftsmen take part. The restaurants prepare dishes such as the *frit de matances amb esclata-sangs*, a sublime combination of pork or lamb tripe with potatoes, vegetables and bloody milk caps. www.ajmancordelavall.net

Parish church of Lloseta

Mancor de la Vall

The church of Sant Pere in Escorca

The church of Sant Llorenç in Selva

PLACES OF INTEREST

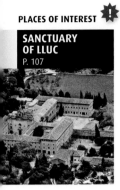

SANCTUARY
OF LLUC
P. 107

The spiritual and identity
centre of Mallorca, where
since the 13th century
they have venerated
the patron saint of the
island, the Mare de Déu
de Lluc, a Gothic stone
sculpture of a black
virgin, according to the
legend found in the
wood by a shepherd.

㉕ ESCORCA

The hamlet gives its name to all the municipality because it was its centre from the 13th to the mid-15th century, when it was transferred to Lluc. As well as a restaurant and the main private houses of the place, the **church of Sant Pere d'Escorca** still stands, that dates back to the 13th century. This is a small church and is one of the churches named as a "repopulation church". This takes us back to the time of Catalan colonization that started in 1230. A rounded keystone arched portal, a pointed diaphragm arch that supports a wooden panel with two slopes and a belfry are just some of the simple elements of this small church.

CELLARS FROM THE
SERRA DE TRAMUNTANA
DIVINS CAN SERVERA
Page **218-219**

㉖ SELVA

This is a municipality on the southern slope of the Serra de Tramuntana in the Raiguer region. The village of Selva occupies the lands of the ancient Islamic farmstead of *Xilvar* and is divided into three centres or historic quarters: in the centre, the Puig of Sant Llorenç, or simply Es Puig, in the northwest, Camarata and in the southwest, Valella.

The parish church of Sant Llorenç is outstanding, with its 14th-century gothic style façade that rises from the top of a monumental stairway. Within the interior, the most valuable treasure is the **Calvari altarpiece** that dates from the second half of the 15th century. Walking enthusiasts of our geography know this village for its traditional connection with the Camí Vell de Lluc.

Apart from this village, **Biniamar**, **Binibona**, **Caimari** and **Moscari** form part of this municipality. They are mountain enclaves that combine tranquillity with the beauty of the landscape and the charm of their traditional architecture.

㉗ CAMPANET

In this municipality, situated at the foot of the Serra de Tramuntana, there are good examples of island architecture, both in the town centre and on the outskirts. Especially outstanding are **Pou d'en Gatell**, on the way out of the town on the Moscari road, **the water trough at Camí Blanc** and **the oratory of Sant Miquel** in Camí Vell de Pollença. One can also visit, after some heavy rain, the **Fonts Ufanes**, sporadic and very powerful springs, resulting from high rainfall in the area and massive filtration of the calcareous rock.

FONTS UFANES

The natural **caves** were discovered in 1945 from a small cavity that was already known to the locals and that was excavated in the search for a spring. The caves that were found are not very large but they have a great aesthetic value and are made up of a route of 400 metres that has beautiful shapes formed by stalactites and stalagmites and a small inner lake. They are outstanding formations, white and very old, like the **Sala Romàntica**, the **Sala del Llac**, the **Castell de les Fades** and the **Cascada Sonora**. There is a scant tourist presence despite the pleasant receptive exterior infrastructure.

The miracle of the Fonts Ufanes occasionally occurs on the Gabellí Petit estate: these are intermittent emergences that spring powerfully and suddenly in the middle of a holm-oak wood after the accumulation of rainwater in the hill or puig Tomir and its environs. The setting has been declared a Natural Monument. To find out if they are active you should check the Council web page.
www.ajcampanet.net

The chapel of Sant Miquel, in Campanet

PLACES OF INTEREST

PUIG DE MARIA
P. 108

The hill or *puig* of Maria is a small elevation (330 m) crowned by a hermitage very close to the heart of the local people, the *pollencins*. There is also a picnic area on the top, an excellent viewpoint, restaurant and guest-house.
www.pollensa.com

② POLLENÇA

The town, a centre with a great cultural and artistic tradition, offers various points of interest, both monumental and urban, that are worth an unhurried visit. We shall start with the **parish church of Nostra Senyora dels Angels** that has a barrel vault. It contains original paintings of the Stations of the Cross above the chapels; the main altarpiece is baroque and one of the chapels has a gothic image of the Mare de Déu. We continue with **Club Pollença**, in the Plaça. This is one of the cultural institutions with the greatest tradition in Pollença. It has a stage area with pictorial contributions that include, amongst others, examples of the Escola Pollencina.

The next stop will be the **old convent of Sant Domingo**, in which the baroque cloister is outstanding. One of the outbuildings of the old convent houses the Museu Municipal de Pollença, inaugurated in 1975, that displays contemporary paintings and gothic paintings from the 15th century. The **Can Desbrull tower** is situated in the Joan March gardens; it is 16th-century and formed part of a stately

CELLARS FROM THE
SERRA DE TRAMUNTANA

**CA'N VIDALET
XALOC**
Page **218-219**

The Plaça Major de Pollença

mansion that was demolished. Returning to the centre, one should pause in front of one of the most popular emblems of Pollença: the **Font del Gall**, in Plaça de l'Almoina, where an iron rooster, the town's heraldic symbol, crowns a base of oval shaped stone.

We shall continue our visit with the **church of Monti-sion**, baroque in style with its old convent that today houses the Town Hall –situated at the foot of the **Calvari** steps, at the top of which there is a chapel dedicated to the Passion. Between 1860 and 1879 a long staircase of 365 steps was built. On the road, more northeast, fourteen Stations of the Cross were placed. Every Good Friday in this setting, the **procession of Davallament** (descent) takes place.

At Nr. 99 Carrer de Costa i Llobera, there is a house called **Can Costa**. This building, of the first half of the 19th century, is the birthplace of the poet Miquel Costa i Llobera; a plaque on its façade commemorates the event. At No. 54 in the same street there is the house of **Can Costa Vell** that dates from the beginning of the 18th century; this has a lintelled portal with a coat of arms and the date 1708. It was owned by Miquel Costa i Llobera's father. We continue

PLACES OF INTEREST

CAP DE FORMENTOR
P. 109

The peninsula of Formentor, which closes the bay of Pollença in the north, is one of the most spectacular and unspoilt spots of the Serra de Tramuntana.

Can Moixet, a café in the Plaça Major

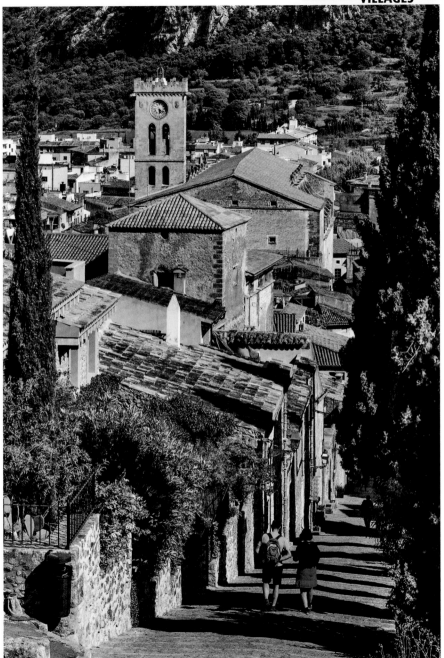

Ascent of the Calvari

our itinerary with the **Chapel of Sant Jordi** that dates from 1532. The chapel is gothic and work was completed on it in 1609.

On the outskirts of Pollença, towards the north, there is the **Pont Romà**. This is a Roman bridge with two arches, with a different typology on its south side, of lowered arch form, whilst the north side is of rounded arch form. Its central part has an emergency drain on the central pillar that seems reinforced in turn by a cutwater that conveys the water towards the two side arches. The upper part of the bridge has a paved floor and side protection walls. Of unknown chronology, it is quite possible that the base that attributed to its tradition and typology is Roman; however, in any case, the bridge was greatly renovated during the Middle Ages. We end this long tour in the **chapel of Roser Vell**. Although its origins could date back to the 13th century, it has been called Roser Vell from the 17th century.

DIONÍS BENNÀSSAR HOUSE-MUSEUM

An 18th-century house where this painter lived half his life, and which shows part of his artistic legacy, personal objects and furniture. It also exhibits the art collection of the Fundació Dionís Bennàssar.
www.museudionisben nassar.com

Roman bridge of Pollença

⁲⁹ PORT DE POLLENÇA

Only six kilometres separate Pollença from the Port and the place has turned into something very different. From an old fishing port leaning towards the bay, it has turned into one of the most cosmopolitan tourist centres in the area. Along the beaches of Gola, Llenaire and Can Cullerassa there are a large number of hotels, restaurants and facilities of every kind and the white sands are surrounded by palm and pine trees. This is a good place to eat fresh fish and to have as a base during one's stay as from here one can discover the area around the natural zone of **S'Albufera**, if we go southeast, to the impressive Cap de Formentor in the north, Cala Sant Vicenç, in the Bòquer valley, or walk along the paths and mountains of the En March valley.

BOAT TRIPS

In summer, from Port de Pollença boats leave daily that cover the bay of Pollença, the cliffs of Formentor or take the route to the beach of Formentor, with a boat leaving hourly.
www.lanchaslagaviota
.com

Pollença bay

Port de Pollença; views of the bay

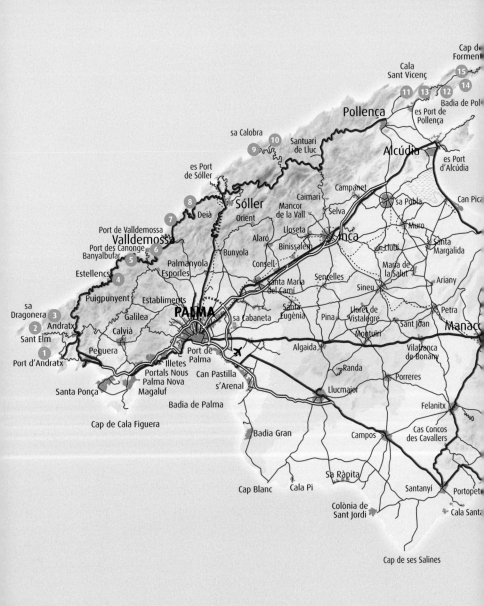

COVES AND BEACHES

Aerial view of Cala Sant Vicenç

❶ CALA D'EGOS

Notwithstanding its relative proximity to Port d'Andratx, this cove remains unspoilt and has no facilities, despite being on an important tourist coast. It is a strip of fine white sand, sheltered by pine trees, that is cut off from a steep and rugged landscape. Access by land is difficult, as the road remains closed to vehicles prior to its end. However, it is possible to reach on foot

Cala d'Egos

or by boat. The crystal clear waters are tinted with blues and greens from the countryside and the sky and there is no development like other points due to difficult access. Being close to Port d'Andratx on the other hand, it is frequented by *llaüts* and some yachts.

❸ CALA EN BASSET

Cala en Basset, a small and sheltered shingle beach of blue waters and not very far from the island of Sa Dragonera, appears, under the spur of La Trapa, to be protected by an old defence tower. It is also one of the unspoilt areas of this coastline, protected against the northwest by the Morro de sa

Cala en Basset

Ratjada. It is not a safe shelter for boats during a storm and access by land is difficult. However, its simple beauty more than compensates the effort to reach it.

❷ BEACH OF SANT ELM AND CALA CONILLS

This strip of sand, shielded by small summerhouses, bears witness to summer leisure activities that have gone on here for many years now. Today, the wide range of facilities available increases the benefits of the area that was dearly loved by the islanders. In winter, the sunsets, broken up by the shadows of the islets of **Pantaleu** and **Sa Dragonera**, make it one of the most appreciated spots of this area. A little further south is **Cala Conills**, with a smaller rocky access, rocks, and little sand, where bathing is even more comforting.

Beach of Sant Elm

④ CALA D'ESTELLENCS

Situated on the right of the point where the Son Fortuny torrent ends, this is a small cove of shingle and pebbles. It forms a seductive and typical retreat where, apart from a refreshing swim in the sea, one can also bathe in the freshwater that flows here. The reeds and fig trees that grow close to the torrent as well as the pine trees close to the sea, soften the sensation of a wild place that the high and reddish walls that fall from the village give. The waters however are deep and clear. A recent jetty and the cave-shaped alcoves that have housed the boats for years confer a certain impression of usefulness on this small beach that is open to nearly all the winds that, be they north or south, come in from the west. Even though it appears to be crammed in the height of the summer, especially at weekends, it becomes an idyllic spot out of season.

⑤ CALA DE BANYALBUFAR

Also known as **S'Arenal**, it is the preferred coastal spot for the people of Banyalbufar. This is a small shingle cove, delimited by high walls, in the middle of which there is a freshwater spring that forms a small waterfall and paints the rock green where it runs down. In the surrounding area one can see the typical huts that house boats. The area is very open to the winds, including the west wind and the north wind; thus it is not recommended to anchor boats here.

The road that descends from the village is short but very steep in order to overcome the notable unevenness of a landscape of old terraced orchards.

Cala d'Estellencs

Boats in the Cala de Banyalbufar

Port des Canonge

Port de Valldemossa

⑥ PORT DES CANONGE

This is a small urbanization established between the 1950's and 1960's that began to expand slowly from the fishermen's huts that already existed. The small access road exit is on the right of the road that goes from Esporles to Banyalbufar at the 80 km point; however the access route on foot from Banyalbufar, via the **Volta des General** (excursion 5, page 160), is highly recommended. Being one of the most sheltered coves from the winds of the area, it provides shelter to numerous boats and one of its charms stems precisely from the multitude of jetties (called *escars* or *alcoves*) that surround the beach. Fishing, formerly carried out here, has now given way to leisure and sports activities, which includes the gastronomic delights of two restaurants. The pinewood environment is a factor that smoothes the beauty of this reddish shingle beach. The very close small beach of **Son Bunyola**, where the torrent ends, is also a stupendous shelter.

S'ESTACA

An old fishermen's village, today for lucky holidaymakers, with access to a tiny cove surrounded by stones, adorned with old escars or huts to keep boats, and clear waters that invite swimming and diving. It is reached via a turning on the right at km 3.9 of the Port de Valldemossa road, where you will find a small car park. You must park the car and continue on foot for 1 hour along a path that drops towards the sea. Along the way you can take in the well-kept estate of S'Estaca, with a house built by the Archduke Ludwig Salvator of Austria in the style of the houses of Lípari, whitewashed and with a flat roof, today owned by the actor Michael Douglas.

⑦ PORT DE VALLDEMOSSA

Little can be said about Port de Valldemossa without reiterating the charm of the small coves that are repeatedly interspersed with the tall cliffs of this slope of the mountain range. Open to the winds, that range from the west wind to the north wind, the harbour can only provide refuge for boats of less than seven metres in length. However, it justifies its name by having been a traditional shelter for fishing boats from Valldemossa. Even though it only has a small breakwater, a few jetties and a small strip of sand and shingle, it is possible to have a good swim here and a restaurant and a collection of summerhouses turn it into a lively spot during the summer season.

⑧ CALA DE DEIÀ

Also very small, with sand, gravel and stones. The colour of its sea-bed is outstanding. Access by car is not recommended in summer, since after dealing with the great unevenness of the road, you must pay to park and at this time of year, there is a great influx of people and it may be full. The best alternative is to go on foot on the **Camí des Ribassos** that goes from the Deià washhouse. The road has been well restored and affords at the same time a pleasant route. One can also go down via the Sa Vinyeta path, which leaves from the northeast area of the village. On the beach there are small dry docks that are characteristic constructions used to remove water or to launch boats; there are also fishing huts and summerhouses. It is also possible to sample good fish in a place that retains an atmosphere of days gone by despite being so crowded. It is near to the beach called **Es Canyeret**, a spot of great beauty in another rocky cove, that one can only reach on foot from the Llucalcari hamlet. For this reason it is less crowded.

TOWER OF SA PEDRISSA
You can get there walking from Cala Deià on a route of about 20 minutes, until reaching the tower of Sa Pedrissa, with views of the coast-line. One of the defence towers that warned of the arrival of enemies is today a magnificent viewpoint.

⑨ CALA TUENT

One of the most heavenly coves in the area, despite being quite built up and frequently visited owing to its proximity to large tourist areas such as **Sa Calobra** and **Torrent de Pareis**. Surrounded by a pinewood and olive trees, its colours transform the waters into a luminous mirror tinted with emerald green, especially at dusk. The beach is of shingle and pebbles, with reddish and golden tones. It is protected by the Morro de sa Corda and the Morro des Forat, Only the mistral and the west winds reach it. There is a restaurant open and sunbed hire is available during the season. The access road is long and winding. However, arriving at the beach becomes an unsurpassable effort award when one finishes the recommended Nr. 10 excursion (see page 183).

Cala de Deià

Cala Tuent

⑩ SA CALOBRA AND TORRENT DE PAREIS

The torrent of Pareis has its source in the confluence of the Albarca or Lluc torrent with the torrent of Gorg Blau, in a point called **L'Entreforc**. In one of the most rugged areas of the Serra de Tramuntana, the torrent flows along a channel of some five kilometres in length, crossing caves, crags, cliffs, pools and freshwater springs, to finally flow into the sea via a bed of sand that closes the backwater called **S'Olla**. This is a small beach of white coarse sand surrounded by tall cliffs that make up one of the most unusual spots in the island.

The descent of the torrent from **L'Entreforc** proves to be very attractive to hikers. However, we have not included it in this guide as it can be quite dangerous unless the descent is carried out in a group with people that have experience of the terrain and the conditions of the route.

The small harbour of **Sa Calobra** is the entrance to the mouth of the torrent by road. It has a few restaurants, other facilities and boats that travel by sea from Sóller. A small track and two tunnels connect this point to the gully. There is also the old access track, a fissure called **Es carrer Nou**.

Its charm results in massive numbers of tourists visiting this spot, so for a more satisfying visit, it is better to come at quieter moments.

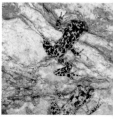

TINY FERRERET

The *Alytes muletensis* lives only in the Torrent de Pareis. It is an amphibian of just 4 cm with a smooth, green skin, and is endemic to the area. The *ferreret*, or Mallorcan midwife toad, today a protected species, was discovered in 1977 from fossilised remains, and in 1981 the first living example was localised.

Entrance tunnel to the Torrent de Pareis

⑪ CALA SANT VICENÇ

This is made up of a group of four coves —Cala Barques, Cala Clara, Cala Molins and Cala Carbó— squeezed together among the tall cliffs of the area. The imposing **Cavall Bernat** mountain range is on the right and the **Punta de Coves Blanques** is on the left. Originally a typical fishing village, it has become a residential area, firstly thanks to islanders who spent their summers here. Today it is a markedly tourist area. The small coves open out to the north and northeast. They have fine white sand and their waters remain tranquil and clear in summer but are awesome when the Tramuntana or Gregal winds blow. At the entrance of the town centre there is a group of seven burial caves of great archaeological value that date from the pretalayotic era, circa 1700 B.C. These are the **l'Alzinaret de Sant Vicenç** caves and there is easy and well signposted access.

⑫ BEACH OF FORMENTOR
(CALA PI DE LA POSADA)

A strip of golden sand, one kilometre in length, it is totally surrounded by pine trees and oaks. There is a background of crystal clear waters, dotted by seaweed and closed to the south by the islet of Formentor. These are the attributes of this cove that paint a wide and precise curve. It is near to the **Hotel Formentor**, that has played host throughout its history to numerous celebrities who, without a doubt, have also appreciated the excellence of this cove.

⑬ CALA BÓQUER

One of the scarce coves that are still virgin today, with more shingle than sand and sometimes covered in mounds of dry seaweed. Its beauty is wild and natural and its landscape is

Cala Bóquer

rounded off by a rural path that leads to it. It is hidden at the foot of the Cavall Bernat mountain range and visiting it means taking a short and beautiful walk from the Bóquer urbanization in the Port of Pollença.

Cala Sant Vicenç

Beach of Formentor (Cala Pi de la Posada)

⑭ CALA MURTA

This cove and the one described below are practically back-to-back, situated as they are on close points but on opposing coastlines of the same Formentor peninsula. Both coves are still virgin. Cala Murta faces east to south and is a good shelter for boats. It is reached from the houses of Cala Murta, at km 12.8 of the road from the Formentor lighthouse (Ma-2210), on the right.

The seabed of the cove is of sand and seaweed and the shingle beach, dotted with pine trees and oaks, form a very valuable natural landscape, interrupted only by the presence of a villa built in the 1950's.

This cove appears in itinerary Nr. 14 (page 205), that goes to the summit of **Fumat**. In the holiday season, youngsters who go to the summer camp in the houses of Cala Murta, that are much higher than the cove, often visit it. The houses are near the lighthouse road and in the middle of the Cala Murta recreational area.

VIEWPOINT OF MAL PAS

At over 200 m above the sea, this is an obligatory stop-off on the way to the Formentor cape, with the best panoramic view over the rocks. It is the work of Antonio Parietti Coll, an engineer who designed the road that goes to the Formentor lighthouse and that of Sa Calobra.

⑮ CALA FIGUERA

As opposed to Cala Murta, this cove faces the northest and the north and is subject to the north wind. The enormous breakwater of **Cap de Catalunya** closes it and from here, up to Cap de Formentor, we can only see tall and imposing cliffs that fall into the sea. The beach is of sand and shingle and the setting is wild and beautiful. The vegetation is basically coastline Mediterranean, steppe, lentisk and reeds. On the right, blackish stone stands out and on the left, marès. On entering the clean waters there is immediate depth for swimming. Access is very easy from km 12.1 of the road that goes to the Formentor lighthouse, on the left, along a narrow track that descends steeply to the sea, in the same cove. We would recommend not using 4x4 vehicles that destroy the track, and show great respect for the Formentor peninsula, a protected area that we wish to maintain at a high level of conservation.

Ornithologists greatly appreciate this setting because It enables them to observe a large variety of birds.

Cala Murta

Cala Figuera

Outlet of the Torrent de Pareis

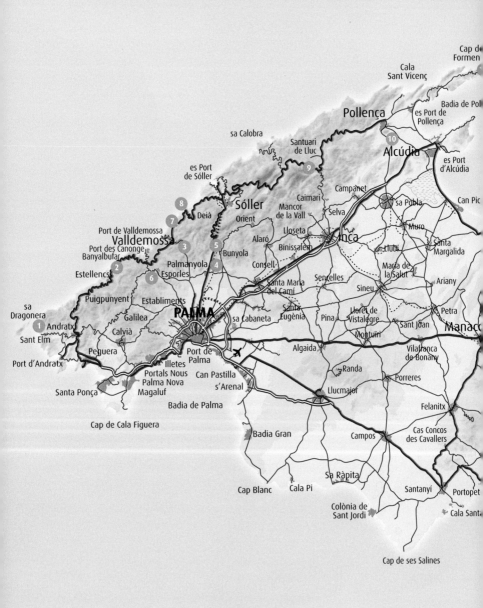

PLACES OF INTEREST

a d'Alcúdia

Cap Ferrutx

ònia de
nt Pere

Artà   Capdepera
              Cala
              Rajada

Son Servera   Canyamel

ant Llorenç   Cala Bona
es Cardassar   Cala Millor

s'Illot

Portocristo

Cala Anguita

les de
allorca

rtocolom

d'Or

1. **LA TRAPA AND SA DRAGONERA**
2. **TALAIA DE SES ÀNIMES (TORRE DES VERGER)**
3. **VALLDEMOSA CHARTERHOUSE**
4. **HOUSES AND GARDENS OF RAIXA**
5. **HOUSES AND GARDENS OF ALFÀBIA**
6. **LA GRANJA (ESPORLES)**
7. **MONASTERY OF MIRAMAR**
8. **SON MARROIG AND SA FORADADA (DEIÀ)**
9. **SANCTUARY OF LLUC**
10. **PUIG DE MARIA**
11. **CAP DE FORMENTOR**

Viewpoint from Mal Pas to Cap de Formentor

❶ LA TRAPA
AND SA DRAGONERA

The property has an area of 74 hectares and the houses situated at a height of 270 metres. The maximum height above sea level is to be found at Puig de la Trapa (472m). At present the property is owned by the **Grup Ornitològic Balear**, who works tirelessly for the conservation of this nature area.

Here an old Trappist monastery stood between 1810 and 1820. Later, from 1853, the same complex of buildings was again used —having been appropriately transformed— as outbuildings for agricultural activities. Until recently the buildings were in ruins, but necessary work has already started on their restoration. One can see remains of the chapel, cells, and monks' workshops, an oven and other outbuildings. The complex of buildings was set around a central patio, open to the east. In the square, opposite the main façade, there presides a magnificent example of an ombú (*Phitolacca dioica*).

Sa Dragonera

From the point of view of traditional engineering, the system of walls and terraces is one of the most interesting elements as is the water system. The region in which La Trapa is located does not have a significant water-bearing stratum that can feed active springs. The solution the Trappist monks gave to the lack of water was to build a complex system of absorption, filtration and collection as well as a later water main to the housing.

Opposite the main building, on the other side of the walls that border the valley, there is an animal driven mill. Further on, we come across an enormous threshing floor and nearby there is a viewpoint from which one can contemplate a magnificent landscape. One needs to proceed with caution, as there is a challenging tall cliff that drops to the sea. At the bottom of the cliff, to the right, one can see **Cala en Basset**, with its rocky beach. Above the cove, on its rocky cape, we can see a defence tower that was built in 1583. From here, one can see before us the island of Sa Dragoneras's southern face: the Llebeig lighthouse, the highest point of Na Popis (360m) with the Far Vell at the top and the Tramuntana cape and lighthouse.

Sa Dragonera has an extended form of approximately four kilometres in length and one in width. Its outline reminds one of a dragon. This seems to explain the origin of its name. The north and northwest parts are very uneven with high cliffs. It contains a rich showcase of endemic flora and fauna. The island passed into public ownership in 1988 and was declared a **Nature Reserve** in 1995. It can be visited by tourist boats that leave from Sant Elm and Port d'Andratx. To go by private boat one needs to apply for permission to the Consell de Mallorca. Disembarking in the natural harbour of **Cala Lladó**, the arrival point, one can visit the most interesting points on foot that are recommended by the visitor's centre.

TALAIA DE SES ÀNIMES (TORRE DES VERGER)

The defence tower dominates the viewpoint

Between Banayalbufar and Estellencs, the Ma-10 road has a rest area at the 88.6 km point. Here one finds the Mirador de ses Ànimes viewpoint, crowned by the watchtower of **Ses Ànimes** or **Torre des Verger**, that keeps watch over the tall cliffs. Built in 1579 by the "Gran i General Consell" in order to defend the coast and the nearby town from incursions by privateers, it became private property at the end of the 19th century.

After a long period in which degradation and obscurity caused the deterioration of the tower, the Govern de les Illes Balears (the Balearic Islands Government) proceeded to restore the tower in 1995, using public funds and thanks to an agreement by the owners to cede the property by 1999. Currently, the **Bany-Al-Bahar** cultural association is working towards public ownership and the maintenance of this emblematic building.

Stopping at this point allows one to contemplate the tower, a symbol of Banyalbufar. However, it also affords spectacular panoramas of the island's north coast. On clear days, one can see up to the western extremity of the **Sa Dragonera** island and make out the light of its lighthouse at dusk. Sunsets are, of course, wonderful. They are one of the best visual gifts provided by nature. Sometimes, for example, when fog sets in on the enclave, one feels as if one is in a magical place.

It is important, when visiting, to park vehicles in the spaces indicated in order not to obstruct the busy mountain road.

③ VALLDEMOSSA CHARTERHOUSE

In Valldemossa one finds the large collection of historic buildings of the Cartoixa de Jesús de Natzaret (Carthusian monastery of Jesus of Nazareth), **La Cartoixa**. This was founded in 1399 on the old residence of the kings of Majorca, called Palau del Rei Sanç. It was secularised in 1835 by the Mendizábal's Disentailment. The first interesting place is the church of La Cartoixa, built between 1751 and 1812. It is neoclassic in style and contains murals by Manuel Bayeu and baroque canvases by Joaquim Juncosa. The main altarpiece has sculptures by Adriá Ferran. After visiting the sacristy, where there are various interesting paintings as well as reliquaries and liturgical objects, we can enter the outbuildings of the new monastery that began to be built in 1717. Let us start with the **Claustre** (cloister) **de les Murteres**, that has four passages covered by arris vaults, and in the uncovered part where there are myrtles

La Cartoixa

(*murteres*) after which the cloister is named. There are also various cypresses and orange trees as well as a baroque fountain in the centre. In one of these passages there is the pharmacy that was moved here in 1933 by Bartomeu Ferrà Joan to the place that was a chapel, from its previous position on a side of the **Pati des Brollador** (the fountain patio). In this pharmacy one can see over a hundred ceramic jars dating from the 18th century, as well as glass containers and other items such as mortars and small scales.

Following along the long south passage of the **Cartoixa Nova** cells, we visit the prior's cell and its chapel, the library, the audience hall, the dining room and the dormitory as well as the garden. These outbuildings house an important artistic, bibliographic and documentary heritage. The route continues with cells 2, which has mementoes of the stay of the writer **George Sand** and the composer **Frédéric Chopin**, such as drawings by Maurice Sand and manuscripts relating to the work *A winter in Majorca*. Cell 4, which is visited independently from the rest of the Cartoixa, is that officially recognised as the Chopion Cell, which features the Pleyel piano.

Chopin's piano

Going on, we can see the different rooms of the **Museu Municipal de Valldemossa** that is divided into four sections: the old Impremta Guasp, with its printing press and various wood engraving blocks; the Archduke Luis Salvador section and the Serra de Tramuntana painter's section that has a great wealth of works of the late 19th century and 20th century.

The fourth section is treated separately as it constitutes the **Museu Municipal d'Art Contemporani** and it has a good collection of paintings by Juli Ramis as well as works by many other contemporary painters such as Joan Miró and Francis Bacon. It also has engravings by Picasso.

From the Cartoixa square, we enter the outbuildings of the so called **Cartoixa Vella**, that happens to be on the same land as the old Palau del Rei Sanç. The first room is the music room that pre-

Interior of the monastery

Library of Prioral Cell of the Cartoixa

serves the pictorial décor of Ricard Anckermann and the subjects are mythology and history. We continue along the 16th-century cloister of Santa Maria and then go up to the dining room of the present **Can Bauçà de Mirabó**, previously known as Can Sureda. This is a product of the adaptations that the old monastery was subjected to from the middle of the 19th century. We now go to hall of the tower, with reminiscences of Gaspar M. de Jovellanos and we can immediately see the rich ornamentation of the Bauçà de Mirabó rooms.

The interior of the **Cartoixa** and the **Palau del Rei Sanç**, as well as the **F. Ghopin and G. Sand Cell**, which requires a separate ticket, can be visited at the times given in the museum section (see page 211). The general visit includes a short concert of the works of Chopin.

④ HOUSES AND GARDENS OF RAIXA

In the municipal district of Bunyola, Raixa was, during the Islamic period, the Araixa farmstead. A personage with great links to **Raixa** was **Cardinal Antoni Despuig** (1745-1813). It was he who reformed the houses into an Italianate classicist style and organized a really notable garden. The houses were reformed in 2007. The entrance portal leads to a large gardened esplanade. On the right one can see a fountain with a relief of three faun heads. What stands out in the patio is the octagonal cistern parapet, with an original stone cover. The chapel contains a baroque altarpiece. In the oil mill, the original implements for crushing olives and a beam press are preserved.

The **lower garden** combines the garden's architecture with the agricultural landscape. In the centre there is a circular fountain and four cypresses that form two tree arches. Also notable are a large

Raixa

The large pond of the Raixa gardens

cactus and an arbour as well as some very tall palm trees. From here, one can contemplate the large arcade of the southern façade.

The entrance to the **upper garden** from the houses is via a classicist portal that has the Despuig family coat of arms on the lintel. Just in front appear the neoclassical steps, in seven sections with different sculptures and ornamental features. There is also a complex irrigation system. The god Apollo presides over the steps on a pedestal on which a mask pours water into a shell. From the bottom part of the steps, along the road on the right, we reach, between cypresses, a pond where there is a very dilapidated sculpture of a mythological character. Behind the pond there is the **Casa en ruïnes** (the house in ruins), the culmination of the romantic atmosphere of the gardens. Along the path on the left is the **Casa de les nines** (the little girl's house). The path heads in the direction of the big **safareig** (open water tank); this is one of the largest in Mallorca. A pavilion, or viewpoint, occupies the upper end of the gardens. The views from here of La Gubia, the Alfabìa mountains, the Comuna de Bunyola, Caubet, the plain and the bay of Palma are magnificent.

Raixa

⑤ HOUSES AND GARDENS OF ALFÀBIA

These are to be found in the municipal district of Bunyola, near to the entrance of the Sóller tunnel. The most outstanding features of the houses are the main façade, the patio and the coffered ceiling of the access to the patio.

The **gardens of Alfàbia** are among the most interesting in Mallorca. From the houses, one goes along a passage that has Tuscan columns and one descends an imperial staircase with balustrades to the first garden. This is a romantic park of the 19th century. A small lake or pond is the centrepiece and this has a fountain in the middle. The wild vegetation, bamboo canes, date palms, palm hearts and other exotic species, create an English style romantic environment.

Inner patio of the houses of Alfàbia

To the north, a pergola with palms leads to what could be called a **baroque garden**. Here there are 32 pairs of columns and more than 24 hydrias that have been converted into delicate fountains. To the east, there is a baroque style square viewpoint with a square stone table. To the west, the pergola ends in a rotunda with eight columns of eight faces. In an unfinished arbor there is a bracken covered fountain that is crowned by the coat of arms of the **Santacília**, with a relief depicting Hercules and the lion of Nemea. There are also Ionic columns and two side bull's eyes. The eastern one (on the left as one leaves the pergola) connects with an interesting barrel vault cistern whilst the western one is the entrance of an old dovecote. From the two leonine figures that flank the base, the stairs descend in paved steps with parallel channels.

The gardens were connected to the water network that originated from the **Verger d'Alfàbia** spring, located on the part of the property that faces northeast, on the Honor road. Apart from the interesting way that the water is carried, Islamic in origin, it is notable by the presence of various flour water-mills.

Alfàbia

Façade of La Granja

⑥ LA GRANJA (ESPORLES)

The houses of the estate of La Granja are situated within the boundary of a very ancient habitat that has been blessed by the presence of an abundant water supply. The first reference we have of the occupation of this space is related to the Islamic farmstead called Alpic. In the land distribution that took place after the Catalan conquest of Jaume I, these lands belonged to the count of Rosselló, **Nuno Sanç**, who gifted them to the Cistercian order in 1233 for the establishment of a monastery. The **Cistercian monks** occupied the ancient farmstead for a short time as a monastery and this was converted into a farm by the **La Real** religious community who were involved in agricultural activities. This explains the origin of the present name, **La Granja** (the farm). From then onwards, the use of water from the present **Font Major**, then called Font de Déu (God's spring), intensified and was the cause of conflicts with neighbouring Esporles. It was later the property of the Vida and Fortuny families.

Architecturally, the houses of La Granja present a complex and irregular layout. This is a result of the additions that were incorporated with the passage of time. The main façade faces northeast, with a wide avenue in front of it that has four large plane trees (*Platanus orientalis*). A baroque coat of arms crowns the portal.

A visit to the houses brings us to spaces and objects of ethnological interest that tell us of the countryside, feudal life and ancient customs. It is a delight to observe, room by room, all the tools that long ago were needed for each trade or entertainments present on the island. It is also a delight to walk around the rock garden, with its waterfall, fountain, statues and romantic grotto. Having finished the visit of the interior, we can now go to see the exterior fountains, the indigenous fauna, a charcoal-burner's hut, the waterfall that comes from the old flour mill and the botanic garden that formerly was an orchard and in which, on certain days of the week, a beautiful folklore show is performed.

La Granja

⑦ MONASTERY OF MIRAMAR

In 1276, **Ramon Llull** founded, in Miramar, a school for oriental languages at which thirteen Franciscan monks were preparing to preach the Gospel and the *Ars luliana* to the non-believers. Once the school had closed, Miramar maintained its importance as a spiritual centre. Subsequently, in 1872, the **Archduke Ludwig Salvator von Habsburg-Lothringen** acquired the property and reformed it, restoring the memory of Ramon Llull and the message of respect and enjoyment of nature by building numerous walkways and viewpoints. Enamoured by these places, he invited the dignitaries of the time to visit. Amongst these was the legendary **Empress Sissi of Austria**, who was so impressed that she named her yacht Miramar.

The place can be visited —today it has been converted into a museum— by firstly passing through the 1934 oil mill, the Archduke's map room, the garden, the **Santa Margalida cloister** (13th centu-

Miramar monastery cloister

ry), close to the portal of the main entrance are some columns from the period of (1276). Now inside, there is a traditional kitchen and objects from the boat of Archduke, the *Nixe II*. One can also see the cenotaph of Vratislav Vyborny, first secretary of the Archduke, from 1879. One needs to enter the **room of the blessed Ramon Llull**, the founder of Miramar, that has various figures that represent his path in life. One continues via the barn and, upon leaving the house, one must head towards the viewpoint, with its beautiful sea views, and the gardens of the **Torre del Moro**, with the Archduke's Italian pond (1872) and the window that came from the Can Burgués palace in Palma, where the Emperor Charles V spent the night in 1541. Further on, we go to the **Jardín de los Cipreses**, in which there are some benches in the shape of Byzantine crosses. We end in the chapel, designed by Friedrich Wachsmann; among other artistic and religious objects, is conserved the triptych of the Trinity and the image of *Notre Dame de la Garde*, a gift from the Empress Sissi of Austria to the Archduke.

Sa Foradada

⑧ SON MARROIG AND SA FORADADA (DEIÀ)

The *possessió* of Son Marroig was known as **La Foradada dels Marroig** prior to the 17th century. Archduke Luis Salvador considered it to be one of the best situated houses in Majorca and wanted to buy it as it was also essential for the archducal project of rebuilding the Lulian Miramar. The transaction did not prove to be easy, but finally he bought it in 1877, paying, however, a far higher price than it was worth. It had 68 hectares and included **Sa Foradada**. Today in Son Marroig, one can visit a small museum dedicated to the Archduke.

One of the most characteristic architectural features is the 16th-century defence tower. It used to protect the houses from the frequent incursions of pirates who would take advantage of the shelter of Sa Foradada to disembark.

Northwest gallery of Son Marroig

The main façade faces northeast. It is three stories high. Inside, the vestibule communicates with the ground floor room that is decorated with beautiful items of furniture and artistic objects, especially old paintings. The main room of the first floor contains most of the **Museu de l'Arxiduc** exhibits. Going on, there is another room that communicates with the northwest gallery, where one can contemplate the fine arches with Tuscan columns and the gallery's balustrade. One also has views from there of Sa Foradada, the pavilion and the coast. From this corridor, stairs descend to the ground floor room where a round arched portal communicates with the rear part of the houses that faces southwest. From a small cobbled avenue there appears a small garden, that is beautifully ornamented, and a small pond. The Archduke undertook major reforms of Son Marroig and added all of the northwest wing where there is the function suite, centred by the already mentioned gallery of five arches. The whole place follows a classicist style with an Italianate flavour.

The famous **Son Marroig viewpoint** is a pavilion of Carrara marble, specifically from Seravezza, that imitates the one on the islet of the Pallavicini garden in Pegli, near Genoa. It stands on a circular base of four steps and is made up of eight Ionic columns. The entablature is sculpturally decorated with bucranes and floral knots. The roof is a semi-spherical dome finished off with a fleuron. From here there is an unbeatable view of the Miramar coast, splendid at sunset.

The **Galliner viewpoint** is made up of two small semicircular towers looking out into emptiness, with stone benches inside the protection wall. From here, the most exceptional landscape feature is the crag of Sa Foradada ("The Holed Stone"). The Archduke liked to say that when he bought the property, he did not even have to pay for the hole.

Garden of Son Marroig

Sa Foradada

Sanctuary of Lluc

The Porxets

Panorama of the Clot d'Albarca

9 SANCTUARY OF LLUC

The Lluc Sanctuary is the spiritual heart of Majorca. Since the 13th century, the image within of the Mare de Déu de Lluc, **patron saint of Mallorca**, has been venerated. In the 15th century the sanctuary was turned into a parish and the administrative centre of Escorca and in time, the nerve centre for religious pilgrimages.

The Mare de Déu de Lluc

From the mid-15th century it was run as a seminary and a choir school was founded, that of the popular **Blauets**. Today, it is maintained by the Missionaries of the Sacred Hearts. A copy of a gothic stele presides over the pilgrim's square, one of the seven couplets of the Mare de Déu that were lined along the Camí d'Inca. There is also a Renaissance fountain and, on the right, the **Porxets**, an interesting example of traditional 17th-century architecture, dedicated to accommodating pilgrims. In the inner patio of the sanctuary there is an image of Bishop Campins, who restored Lluc at the beginning of the 20th century, and the church façade that was modified in the 1920s. Theinterior of the church is early baroque and dates from 1620. There is an altarpiece by Jaume Blanquer, a gothic sculpture in dark stone that depicts the image of the Mare de Déu.

The **Museu de Lluc** has a wealth of archaeological exhibits of items discovered in the nearby burial cave called **Sa Cometa des Morts**, the donated treasures of the Mare de Déu, typical Mallorcan clothing and religious garments, medieval and modern religious images, ceramics and paintings from the 18th and 19th centuries, most of them from the Mulet collection, as well as the collections of the painters Josep Coll Bardolet and Guillem Gil.

The **Camí dels Misteris** rises to the top of the Trobada hill and appears adorned by five sculpture collections that include the fifteen mysteries of the Rosary. They were designed by Joan Rubió and Guillem Reinés (1909) and incorporated the bronze medallions made by the sculptor Josep Llimona.

⑩ PUIG DE MARIA

This protected area of 67 hectares (Nature Area of Special Interest) is crowned by the summit of the Puig (333 metres) that became the historical and religious centre of the Pollença area. **The Mare de Déu des Puig** sanctuary, known to exist since the middle of the 14th century, was one of the most important on the island. Today it has been converted into an inn that also serves food. It is worth spending at least one night there in order to enjoy the dawn from this excellent spot and to contemplate the wide Pollença bay.

The last stretch of hillside of almost one kilometre has to be under-taken on foot. It is a beautiful paved road between dry-stone walls. Once getting to the top, one comes across a large complex of build-ings, amongst which stand out the defence tower, the walls, that protect the monastery, the church and the gothic style refectory. One can also see the ruins of an old flour mill and a collection of wells and cisterns that collected rainwater.

The ascent to the top is of exceptional beauty. Apart from the views over the bay, the capes of **Formentor** and **Pinar** and the Sant Vinceç valley, one can observe the geological diversity of the Puig. This includes plenty of caves and pot-holes and the wealth of vegetation that sur-rounds it, especially a dense oak wood and many species of brushwood. There are also many visiting birds such as sparrows, green-finches and goldfinches, amongst others.

Outline of the Puig de Maria

⑪ CAP DE FORMENTOR

The Formentor peninsula stretches some 12 kilometres to the northeast and reaches 3 kilometres in width. It has a rugged relief with heights such as the Pal (423m), the Talaia d'Albercutx (380 m) and the Fumat (334m). It is one of the most spectacular areas of the Serra de Tramuntana and it possesses an extreme and wild beauty. Designated as **ANEI** (Nature Area of Special Interest) **de Formentor i Cavall Bernat**, it has, at its base, the urbanization of the Port de Pollença, where, notwithstanding the incredible growth in tourism, it is still possible to see fishermen's houses and summerhouses that date from the beginning of the 20th century; it starts to rapidly gain height however against the shelter of the sharp Cavall Bernat mountain range. The outline of these mountains encloses the wonderful **Bóquer valley** and the cove of the same name. Along the Formentor road (Ma-2210), at km 5.5 leaves the access way to the elevated **Talaia d'Albercutx** and on the left there appears the spectacular

Cap de Formentor, with the road and the lighthouse

viewpoint called **Mal Pas** or **La Creueta**, that faces out to the tall cliffs and the **islet El Colomer**.

Then, on the western side, one finds the beach of Formentor or the **Pi de la Posada** cove that has a sandy beach enclosed by dunes, a pine wood and oak trees and sheltered by the island of Formentor that has tourist facilities in summer although it has not been developed with the exception of the **Hotel Formentor**. Built in 1929, it has been a centre of international renown insofar as celebrated figures from the world of art, politics and show business have stayed there over the many years of its existence.

Other points of interest on the Formentor peninsula are to be found in the **recreation area of Cala Murta**. The tarmac road starts at the 12.8 km point and is equipped with tables, benches and barbecue areas. These are used less in summer though, when making fires is prohibited because of the fire risks. At its highest point we can see an oak wood and a pine wood as well as many rosemary shrubs and heather; we find the houses of the estate of **Cala Murta**, formerly owned by the Costa i Llobera family. The estate is of great ethnological value and today houses the Rotger-Villalonga Foundation that promotes the life and work of the poet. It is also fitted out as a summer camp. Very close are the transparent waters of **Cala Murta. Cala en Gossalba** is further north and is less frequented due to difficult access.

The **Camí Vell del Far** starts at Cala Murta. It was built in the mid- 19th century and its development is described in the Fumat excursion (itinerary Nr. 14, page 205). Before (km 12.1 of the road, on the left) the path starts that takes us to **Cala Figuera**, one of the virgin coves that we have mentioned previously.

A little further on, the road goes through a tunnel and takes us, with twists and turns and unevenness, to the Cap de Formentor point where there is the imposing structure of the lighthouse. This enclave is the most northerly geographical point in all of the island of Mallorca. The sensation felt here is inexplicable, with a high view of the immense sea and the jagged coast that allows us, on clear days, to see the neighbouring island of Minorca.

The poem of **Miquel Costa i Llobera** describes, with great skill, the wild landscape and spirit of Formentor; it is highly recommended to read the poem prior to taking this beautiful route.

Dusk at the Mirador del Mal Pas or of La Crueta

Panorama of Cap de Formentor

CAR TOURS

d'Alcúdia

Cap Ferrutx

ia de
Pére

rtà Capdepera
Cala
Rajada

Son Servera Canyamel

it Llorenç Cala Bona
i Cardassar Cala Millor

s'Illot

Portocristo

Cala Anguita

es de
lorca

ocolom

'Or

1 **PALMA** → CAMP DE MAR → PORT D'ANDRATX →
ANDRATX → S'ARRACÓ → SANT ELM → ESTELLENCS →
BANYALBUFAR → ESPORLES → **PALMA**

2 **PALMA** → CALVIÀ → ES CAPDELLÀ → GALILEA →
PUIGPUNYENT → ESPORLES → **PALMA**

3 **PALMA** → VALLDEMOSSA AND ES PORT → DEIÀ →
LLUCALCARI → SÓLLER → PORT DE SÓLLER → BINIARAIX →
FORNALUTX → **PALMA**

4 **PALMA** → BUNYOLA → ORIENT → ALARÓ →
BINISSALEM → CONSELL → SANTA MARIA → **PALMA**

5 **PALMA** → SÓLLER → SA CALOBRA → ESCORCA →
SELVA → INCA → **PALMA**

6 **INCA** → SANCTUARY OF LLUC → POLLENÇA →
CALA SANT VICENÇ → PORT DE POLLENÇA → **FORMENTOR**

El Penyal des Migdia from Puig Major

PALMA → CAMP DE MAR → PORT D'ANDRATX → ANDRATX →
S'ARRACÓ → SANT ELM → ESTELLENCS → BANYALBUFAR →
ESPORLES → **PALMA**

Interest: **Landscape**

One needs to leave Palma by the western dual carriageway (Ma-1).
Upon entering the municipal area of Calvià we see, on the left, the
neo-gothic castle of **Bendinat**. The new dual carriageway continues
past Palmanova towards the Andratx road. On the right is the neo-
Romanesque chapel of the **Pedra Sagrada** that reminds us that
these landscapes were the scene of the conquest of 1229. Then we
pass around the Santa Ponça junction where there is a typical windmill on the right and further on, we pass the tourist resort of
Peguera on one side whilst the road goes through the tunnels of Son
Vic. A road that goes to the left leads to another tourist resort, **Camp
de Mar**, that has a beautiful beach, whilst the main road approaches
the pass that gives way to the Garrafa mountain on the right. Just at
the entrance of Andratx, the same road (Ma-1) turns to the left and

leads to **Port d'Andratx**. The cove of the port, closed off at the southwest by Cap de la Mola, appears to be very built-up, with plenty of luxury homes. However, there are still beautiful spots such as the **Torrent del Saluet**.

We go back to the same road in the direction of **Andratx**, and after having visited this town, we head west on the S'Arracó and Sant Elm road (Ma-1030). The small village of **S'Arracó** is worth a visit, including the environs of the church. On the road to Sant Elm, we go past the S'Arracó cemetery and cross the Palomera pass. A few more kilometres of tarmac along mountain landscapes leads us to the entrance of **Sant Elm**, which has a beautiful beach that is presided over by the outline of the **Es Pantaleu** islet and, as a backdrop, the immense crest of **Sa Dragonera**. To the left of the town centre there is the old tower and the sailor's chapel, dedicated to the saint who gives his name to this place. On the right there is the small jetty for the Sa Dragonera boat that offers an interesting angle in the contemplation of the landscape as well as access to the island.

We now return towards Andratx, where we need to take the Serra de Tramuntana road (Ma-10) that in a north-north-westerly direction will lead us to **Estellencs**. First we pass next to the **Torre de Son Mas**, that is today the seat of the Andratx Town Hall. The road goes up to the Sa Gramola pass, from which starts the **La Trapa** path. It opens up a view of the northern coast that is on the left,

Port d'Andratx

whilst on the right there are the wild slopes of the Mola de s'Esclop. At its lower part, the coast portrays idyllic spots such as **Caló de ses Ortigues**. Continuing on the road, we reach **Es Grau**, that has a bar/restaurant with a spacious terrace, and the small viewpoint dedicated to **Ricard Roca**. Below is the En Pruaga beach that has a difficult access.

Next, at the Ma-10, 97 km point, there is a road on the right that goes up to the **Área Recreativa Natural de Ses Serveres** (Son Fortuny). After passing the Mirador des Coll des Pi, the road descends to the small village of **Estellencs**, that clings to the slopes of the Puig de Galatzó and looks out to sea. One has to admire the church steeple, the small uneven alleys and the reddish stone steps. One should also go for a stroll towards **Cala d'Estellencs**.

From Estellencs to **Banyalbufar**, the road offers exceptional views, where the sea and the mountains combine their charms and achieve top quality landscape heights. Country houses such as Es Collet and Son Serralta and terraced lands appear on the route. After Punta de Son Serralta, we enter the municipal district of Banyalbufar, with the large property of publicly-owned **Planícia** on the right. Finally, we reach an emblematic point of the landscape of the north coast (Costa Nord), the Torre des Verger or **Talaia de les Ànimes**, with its watchtower that dates back from the end of the 16th century. There is also an exceptional view that stretches southeast to Sa Dragonera, and to **Sa Foradada** in the northeast and to the Sóller mountains. One could say that the terraces appear to fall into the sea; a small path leads to the coastal corner of **Pedra de s'Ase**. Banyalbufar, a village embroidered by terraces, is an example of laborious mountain farming. The entrance patio of **La Baronia** and the town square are not to be missed visits; the boldest visitors climb the steep streets... or they descend towards Cala Banyalbufar.

Upon leaving Banyalbufar, we leave the **Volta des General** and the Baix de Son Bunyola track that is used for going to Port des Canonge on foot, and we go up the saddle of Sa Bastida, that affords views of **Son Bunyola** and **Port des Canonge**, a residential enclave that has its own road some kilometres further after the houses of the estate of Son Valentí. Leaving the views over the coast, the road reaches an important intersection where the Ma-10 mountain road contin-

Talaia de les Ànimes

ues towards the left in the direction of Valldemossa, whilst our route turns towards the right to Esporles (Ma-1100). Descending the tarmac, we follow the excursion route called **Camí des Correu**. Later, on the right, close to the Puigpunyent road, there lies the house/museum of **La Granja**. This is of great historical, architectural and ethnological interest. Between La Granja and Esporles, one is surprised by the splendid vegetation of the Esporles torrent, with its poplars, ashes and, further on, its great collection of plane trees (*Platanus Orientalis*), that have a golden reflection in autumn. We enter **Esporles** by the narrow road of Badaluc and we leave the car in order to wander along the village's main street.

After Esporles, we suggest that the return to Palma be made by the old road (Ma-1040) that goes up to Coll d'en Portell and then descends towards the centre of Establiments, an independent village for decades until it was joined to Palma. From Rutló, the centre of **Establiments**, with the walls of Son Berga on the left, we head towards Palma via Secar de la Real.

CAR TOUR 2

PALMA → CALVIÀ → ES CAPDELLÀ → GALILEA →
PUIGPUNYENT → ESPORLES → **PALMA**

Interest: **Landscape**

We leave Palma and head towards the Coll de sa Creu (Ma-1043)
that crosses the Serra de na Burguesa. In order to do this, we go to
the roundabout that is near the military base of Son Suredeta
(close to Gènova), which we reach easily via Carrer Andrea Doria
or the ring-road, taking the Gènova exit. Narrow and winding, the
road rises above the 340m height of the Coll de sa Creu after having passed close to the houses of Santa Eulàlia that are on military-
owned land. Between **Coll de sa Creu** and Coll del Vent, already
in the municipal district of Calvià, we can see some of the most
representative landscapes of the **Serra de na Burguesa**; there is a
hunter's shelter and roads to cross on foot, such as the one that
goes to the **Mirador de n'Alzamora**. Immediately afterwards the
road descends towards Valldurgent; the houses of the estate have a
long history. Having passed the houses, we join the road that

comes from Establiments (Ma-1016) and turn to the left in the direction of Calvià.

On both sides properties appear, such as Es Burotell, Benàtiga —Vell and Nou— and Son Boronat. Immediately afterwards on the left, at the top of the hill, are the houses of **Son Roig**. A little further along, we enter the town of **Calvià**, the centre of the tourist and cosmopolitan district of the same name, that, however, retains the characteristics of an essentially rural village. From the town of Calvià, we follow the **Es Capdellà** road (Ma-1015); it is the rural village of the same district that we reach in a short time. Its tranquil alleys welcome us and its backdrop is the Puig de Galatzó.

Before reaching the road that goes from Es Capdellá to Andratx and turn to the northeast, on the right, on the Galilea and Puigpuny-ent road (Ma-1032). We pass next to large estates such as Son Claret —with its battlement towers and currently a hotel—, Galatzó and Son Martí, then we climb up a mountain road in search of **Galilea**, that, as its name suggests, resembles a nativity scene village. The houses are spread out on a slope, on the left of the road, above ter-

races that defy the sloping hillside. A stroll on foot, with the church square as a refer-ence point, will give us a break from the kilometres of tarmac.

From Galilea we go down towards **Puig-punyent**, after having gone past the Coll des Molí de Vent, with the Son Cortei prop-erty and the considerable Puig de na Bauça-na on the right and followed by the smallholdings of Conques. Prior to entering Puigpunyent, a road on the left goes up to one of the footpaths for climbing up the Puig de Galatzó and the **Reserva de Galatzó**, a private nature reserve. Once in Puigpunyent, we cross its urban area, firstly via the **Vila** quarter with the Palma road

Puig de Galatzó

that heads towards the right. We leave this road to one side as we have to go straight. Then we pass through **Serral** and the **Son Bru** district at whose end is the Esporles road (Ma-1101).

We leave Puigpunyent and on the left there is the Camí Vell d'Estellencs, in the vicinity of Son Fortesa. The road gains height and on the left we can see the **Puig de na Fàtima**, that is full of magical legends; the very narrow road continues and reaches the Coll des Grau, the entrance door to the Superna valley that affords beautiful landscapes on the stretch that goes from Mola de Planícia to the Fita del Ram. The properties of Son Noguera and Son Vic give access to the Esporles municipal district; prior to the Banyalbufar intersection, we can see the house-museum of **La Granja**. We turn to the right in the direction of **Esporles** on the Ma-1100 road that runs next to the torrent and we arrive into the village after a few minutes.

We return to Palma on the Ma-1120 road that links up with the Valldemossa road. Before, at the exit of the village, we leave behind on the right the old road via Establiments (see route by car 1). On the left of our landscape the outline of the **Mola de Son Pacs** takes shape, whilst on the right there are the houses of an old and large *possessió*, Canet. Near to S'Esgleieta we take the Valldemossa to Palma road. Along flat ground, we pass next to the university campus and a few kilometres later, we enter the capital.

Small-spotted Genet (*Genetta genetta*)

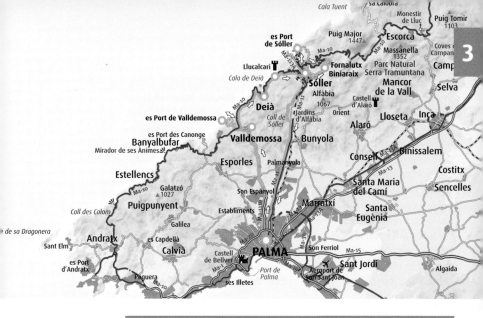

CAR TOUR 3

PALMA → VALLDEMOSSA→ PORT DE VALLDEMOSSA→ DEIÀ →
LLUCALCARI → SÓLLER → PORT DE SÓLLER → BINIARAIX →
FORNALUTX → **PALMA**

Interest: **Landscape, historical and monumental**

We leave Palma by the Valldemossa road (Ma-1110). After the Universitat de les Illes Balears campus and the small village of S'Esgleieta, olive trees dominate the landscape and the road rises rapidly towards S'Estret, between the crags of the Puig de na Fàtima, on the right, and the foothills of the Mola de Son Pacs, on the left. Beyond S'Estret, there appears the beautiful **valley of Son Matge**, at the threshold of Valldemossa, a town that magnificently stretches out on our left. After the bend at Sa Coma, we reach the town centre. The town of **Valldemossa** is a cultural centre of the first order, dominated by the old **Carthusian monastery**.

From Valldemossa we head towards the Pollença-Andratx road (Ma-10), along a short stretch of road that takes us to the intersection of this important road link of the Serra de Tramuntana, with the houses of the estate of Son Moragues on the right. The way leading to Deià continues on our right, but for now, we turn left if we want to see the **Port de Valldemossa** and take the Ma-10 road towards Andratx. One needs to proceed with care because less than half a kilometre along the road one needs to turn right to take the port road. The first stretch runs along the Pla del Rei and the talayotic shrine of **Son Mas** on the left. Just afterwards, on the right, there are the houses of the estate of Son Mas with a defence tower. From here, the road descends vertiginously towards the sea, with the deep hollow of the Torrent des Port or Marina on the left. The Port de Valldemossa has a small centre of houses that are essentially second homes and a few older fishing huts. The breakwater of the pier protects a few boats and there is also a restaurant. We leave behind the narrow port road and get back to the Ma-10 road, that now we take towards the left, leaving the Valldemossa intersection on the right, in order to head towards Deià. At the 69.8 km point there is a road that goes up to the **Trinitat chapel**, founded in 1648 by Joan Mir de la Concepció.

Carrer de Sa Lluna, Sóller

From Can Costa to the Pedrissa property, just before Deià (km 61), the Archducal **Miramar** coast stretches out. Nearby, the **Mirador de la Vorera**, a small neo-Arabic inspired tower, stands out. Further on, to the right, there is the house of Son Galcerán and, on the left, the **Talaia de Trinitat** or ses Pites, a watchtower erected at the beginning of the 17th century that formed part of the Mallorcan defence circuit. Next follows the modern hotel that occupies the site of the old Archducal inn called **Ca Madò Pilla**. Before the hotel, on the left of the road, there is the **Pi** or **Niu des Corb viewpoint**, from where one can contemplate the coast that surrounds the houses of the estate of **S'Estaca**, that the Archduke had built in the Sicilian style.

There follows on the left the **Miramar** *possessió*, previously mentioned as a Lulian and Archducal centre. It preserves the defence tower, that has a square ground plan, the chapel and the gothic arch that came from the old convent of Santa Margalida in Palma.

After Miramar we enter the municipal district of **Deià**. On the right are the houses of the estate of Son Gallard, a property linked to the life of **Santa Catalina Tomàs**, as the niche of the Valldemossa saint reminds us. Further ahead, on the left, there are the houses of the estate of **Son Marroig**, from where one can contemplate the beautiful image of **Sa Foradada**. Of the country house, the square ground plan defence tower stands out, with its Renaissance windows that were added in the 19th century. Also outstanding is the west gallery that dates from the time of the Archduke and **the viewpoint** that is shaped like a classical small temple, with a circular ground plan and built of Carrara marble. The interior of the houses include a small Archducal themed museum, that exhibits furniture, ceramics, books, archaeological items and paintings that belonged to the Archduke. The coast of the large Miramar continues even after Son Marroig, along the **Sa Pedrissa** property, close to Deià, that has a late 17th century defence tower.

After Sa Pedrissa the visitor will have the small village of **Deià** in sight, with its church towering on a hill and the imposing rocky wall of the Puig des Teix massif in the form of a buttress. Deià is a place with its roots in the landscape; it is a meeting point for artists and intellectuals, such as the writer Robert Graves. The ascent to the church affords us the double spectacle of the magnificent landscape and the group of houses that are a good example of traditional mountain architecture.

After Deià, we leave, on the left, the **Cala de Deià** road and, on the right, **Ca n'Alluny**, the house-museum dedicated to Robert Graves, which is worth a visit. Further on, on the right the Ca l'Abat road rises. We see on our left the **Llucalcari** hamlet that has some fortified houses and a defence tower. A little further on, having left the view above the coast, there appears the panoramic view over the **Sóller valley**, that is at the foot of the highest mountains in the island. After a few kilometers of twists and turns between olive groves, we enter the town of Sóller, surrounded by orchards and

Plaça de la Constitució, Sóller

orange groves. **Sóller**, a trading and agricultural town, possesses a rich artistic heritage, with large traditional and modernist houses and a large baroque and modernist church.

The Port de Sóller is very near Sóller, only three kilometres away on the final stretch of the Ma-11 road from Palma, and at this point becomes the Ma-1134. We pass by the **L'Horta** area, with its houses scattered amongst the orange trees; we leave, on the right, the continuation of the mountain road (Ma-10) that goes towards Lluc and we continue, passing next to the monument that recalls the battle between the inhabitants of Sóller and the Islamic pirates in 1561, to arrive a short time later at the port. It is a rather unusually shaped bay, almost circular, with its perimeter filled largely by hotels and different buildings. It is highly recommended to make use of the already typical tram, parking your car, to experience this short journey that is sensational, the large tourist influx permitting, of course! From the port, it is also interesting to head for **Sa Calobra** and the **Torrent de Pareis** in the boats that make this short trip. Once having visited the enclave, we return to Sóller.

We leave the town by the Carrer de Sa Lluna and we soon after pass the place called L'Alqueria des Comte to then reach the pictur-

Interior of the Bàlitx d'Avall country hotel

esque village of **Biniaraix**, at the foot of the Ofre gully. Its paved streets are worth a gentle stroll along them, seeing the unsmooth stone houses, with a few painted tiled eaves; one should also take a look at the **gully of Biniaraix** once past the public wash house. Here starts a magnificent paved and stepped road that scales the heights. From a narrow road that starts near the wash house, we can join up directly with the road that links Sóller to **Fornalutx** to get closer to this last town that is an example of an urban centre with a mountain landscape.

From Fornalutx we return directly to Sóller, with Biniaraix on the left and Binibassí on the right. On the outskirts of Sóller we take the Ma-11 road in order to return to Palma via the toll tunnel that bores through the Alfàbia mountain range —still a toll payment in 2017— or through the twists and turns of the Coll de Sóller, a winding road with interesting landscapes.

Sa Calobra

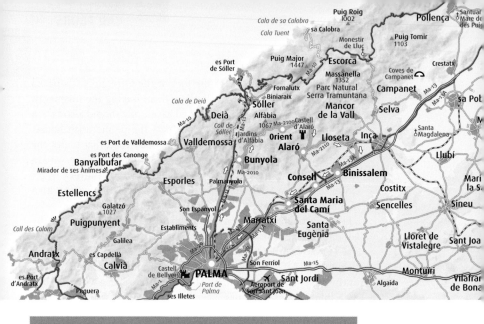

One sets off from Palma on the Sóller road (Ma-11). After Palmanyola and the roundabout of S'Esgleieta to the Santa Maria road, on
the left, at the 12.2 km point, there are the **Raixa** and **Biniatzar**
properties at the foot of the mountain. Both *possessions* were, in
olden times, Islamic farmsteads. Having passed the 14 km point, we
leave the Sóller road and turn to the right, along a stretch of the
road (Ma-2010) that takes us quickly to **Bunyola**.

After visiting Bunyola, with its small streets that climb the lowest
slopes of Comuna, we go to Orient on the Ma-2100 road. Along this
route we see estate houses, such as Son Creus at the 2.5 km point
and mountain landscapes that were brilliantly described by **Llorenç
Villalonga**. The road proceeds along narrow bends and reaches the
Coll d'Honor and the Penyals d'Honor, the highest point of the
Comuna de Bunyola, that dominates our right, whilst the **Serra
d'Alfàbia** rises on our left.

Having gone beyond the pass, the road twists down very rapidly towards the idyllic **Orient valley**. On the right there is the setting of **Es Freu**, that connects with the Coanegra road. Devouring more tarmac, we see that on the left there is the old Lluc to Son Vidal and Coma-sema road. A little further, at the 10 km point, we enter the small village of Orient, one of the most typical in the mountains of Mallorca. There are good bar and restaurant facilities and the church of Sant Jordi protects this setting.

From Orient we go towards Alaró, still surrounded by beautiful mountain landscapes. The large *possessió* of **Solleric** appears on the left (at the 14.2 km point), whilst on the right the crags of the **Puig del Castell d'Alaró** rise. A little further on, the road passes between two large hillocks, almost twins, on the right the aforementioned **des Castell** and the other, on the left, the **Puig de l'Alcadena**. Prior to entering Alaró one could turn left to link up with the small Lloseta road (Ma-2110). However, it is more advisable to continue towards **Alaró** in order to get to know this village, with its interesting architectural works; many of them, like the church and the

Strawberry trees

Town Hall, both in the same square, show a great skill in the use of exposed stone.

From Alarò we continue in the direction of Lloseta on the Ma-2110 road and we find, after Son Grau, the area of **Tofla** that is also very much connected with the work of Llorenç Villalonga. On the right there is a good view over Can Sec de Tofla and the crag of Can Jeroni. Close to the 6 km point of the road, there is a road on the left that affords an optional view of the area of **Clot d'Almadrà**, a magnificent valley surrounded by high mountains. Heading once again towards **Lloseta**, the Raiguer road (on the right, towards the 4.7 km point) will lead us to Binissalem along the Morneta property.

However, we recommend turning left in order to visit the village of Lloseta, with monuments such as the **Palau d'Aiamans** and, on the outskirts, the **chapel of Cocó**. We can reach Binissalem by the direct road that sets off towards the southwest after the chapel or by the small road (Ma-2111) that links up with the Inca road (Ma-13A) opposite the **Foro de Mallorca** (that has a wax museum on the history of Majorca and other attractions). Although it does not form part of the Serra de Tramuntana region, **Binissalem** is worth a long visit, especially for its architectural heritage and one should not forget that it is the centre of the most important wine-growing area in Majorca.

We continue from Binissalem along the old Inca to Palma road (Ma-13A) and we pass the village of **Consell** that has a crafts tradition. Next we reach **Santa Maria del Camí**, with its interesting monuments, such as the Town Hall, cloister of the old Mínimos convent and the parish church as well as the landscape area of the **Coanegra valley**. We can reach Palma by the old road, thus catching a glimpse of the landscape of the Marratxí municipality, both rural and urban owing to the demographic increase that has been the result of its proximity to the capital.

Ses Fonts Ufanes

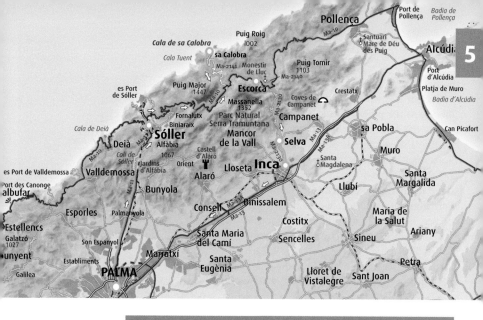

CAR TOUR 5

PALMA → SÓLLER → SA CALOBRA → ESCORCA →
SELVA → INCA →**PALMA**

Interest: **Landscape**

We leave Palma on the Sóller road (Ma-11). After Palmanyola and the roundabout of the S'Esgleieta to Santa Maria road, there are, on the left, the *possessions* of **Raixa** and **Biniatzar**, at the foot of the mountain. We leave the Bunyola road on the right and pass Can Penasso, an old farm worker's boarding house, on the right, whilst on the left there appear the large houses of **S'Alqueria d'Avall**. Carrying on along the road, just before the tunnel that crosses the Serra d'Alfàbia, we come across, on the right, the houses and **gardens of Alfàbia**, an example of an ancient Islamic farmstead that preserves gothic, mudejar and, especially, baroque elements as well as the spectacular baroque and romantic gardens. A visit (there is an admission fee) is highly recommended.

After Alfàbia, there appears the toll tunnel of Sóller that penetrates the mountain for three kilometres. There is also the possibility of

**The descent down
to Sa Calobra**

going up the traditional road of Coll de
Sóller but this would make the route much
longer. At the other end of the tunnel there
awaits the formidable **Sóller valley**. After
visiting this mountain capital, we take the
Port road and, prior to arriving, we turn
right on the Ma-10 road that goes up the
slope of the mountain. Leaving behind the
Fornalutx intersection, we pass the Mirador
de Ses Barques, a not to be missed stop-off
for contemplating the view over the Port de
Sóller. The route goes up along the escarp-
ment of the Penyal des Migdia, of the Puig Major massif, and crosses
the Son Torrella mountains via a short tunnel, after which, already in
the Escorca district, it leads us to the reservoirs of **Cúber** and **Gorg
Blau** amongst landscapes of the high mountains of Mallorca. Next to
Gorg Blau, a column reminds us that in this place there used to be
the Talayotic sanctuary of **Almallutx**. Further on, after the Turixant
tunnel, there sets off, to the left, the tortuous road that leads to **Sa
Calobra** and the mouth of the **Torrent de Pareis**. The Sa Calobra
road (Ma-2141) passes through 700 metres of unevenness in 13 kilometres of continuous bends. It is the road with the most number of
bends in all Mallorca, something to bear very much in mind prior to
taking the double journey of descent and ascent. One can alter the
route we present here by returning from Sa Calobra to Sóller by boat,
always, of course, having arranged this in advance. The Sa Calobra
road goes up initially to the Coll de Cals Reis and reaches the curious
Nus de sa Corbata (tie-knot), where it interweaves with itself and
then it launches itself on a vertiginous descent of hairpin bends.
Meanwhile, the calcareous landscape continues to impress.

Already much further down, we pass next to the Es Bosc house and
through crags that have capricious appearances, such as
Cavall Bernat. Immediately after there is a road that goes to the left
and takes one to the interesting spot of **Tuent**. The hamlet
of Sa Calobra, made up of little more than eight houses, is on the left
of the road that later reaches the **cove of Sa Calobra** that is on a coast
where sea and mountains are united. There are also various restau-

rants and shops. It is de rigeur to take the walk that, after the pedestrian tunnel leads to the mouth of the **Torrent de Pareis**, a marvel of nature in which the karst erosion acquires its maximum expression.

After the amazing stretch of this road that goes down to Sa Calobra and the visit to the Torrent de Pareis, one needs to undertake the return ascent, something that should be undertaken with all the calm in the world. When we are again at the intersection with the Ma-10 road, we turn to the left in the direction of Escorca and Lluc. One passes under an old hydroelectric aqueduct and, on the left, we see the rugged landscape that surrounds the Gorg Blau torrent on the stretch known as **Sa Fosca**. The road passes the **Pareis torrent viewpoint**, a good spot to contemplate the karst ravine that rapidly flows towards the sea. Immediately after, we reach the hamlet of **Escorca**. Four kilometres further we reach the Coll de sa Batalla, at whose start there is the junction of the Inca road (Ma-2130) that we follow to the right, leaving the road that, on the left, continues via a detour to Lluc (Ma-2140) or that reaches Pollença via the Ma-10 road.

Puig Major

From the hill along the Ma-2130 road, we continue on the constant descent, round tight bends. Halfway down, one passes the **Bretxa Nova**, an incredible split in the rock, on whose high part was the legendary **Salt de la Bella Dona** pass (jump of the beautiful lady). A little further on we reach the Barracar, an old pilgrim's boarding house that today is privately owned. Further below, olive trees start to dominate the landscape. We pass through the small village of **Caimari** and, a little later on, we reach **Selva**.

From Selva to Inca the road (Ma-2114) runs through fields that already come under the Raiguer region. We practically enter the centre of Inca by turning right at the Palma-Alcúdia road (Ma-13A), on which we continue heading south towards Palma. On the outskirts of Inca one can opt between continuing on the (Ma-13A) road or going on the motorway (Ma-13) in order to once again enter Palma, the end of the journey.

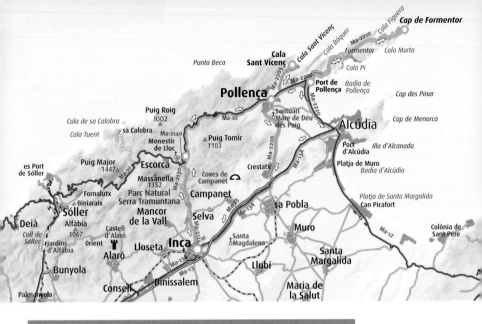

INCA ↘ SANCTUARY OF LLUC ↘ POLLENÇA ↘
CALA SANT VICENÇ ↘ PORT DE POLLENÇA ↘ **FORMENTOR**

Interest: **Landscape, historical and monumental**

From Palma we go towards **Inca** on the Ma-13 motorway. We enter Inca and, by the old road (Ma-13A), towards the right we approach the next roundabout, where we turn left and cross the town centre to link up with the Lluc road (Ma-2114 and then Ma-2130). The image of **Selva**, of which stands out the bell tower, continues to become closer. The centre of the town is on the left and, past the cemetery, the road begins a descent to Caimari. This small village can be entered via the entrance door prior to the imposing walls of the mountains. The road crosses Caimari and penetrates the mountain landscape, with its olive tree terraces and details such as the curious **Rota des Carter** hut, built next to a large rock that integrates into the building. On the left, the view is dominated by the pointed Puig de n'Escuder. In the meantime, the Camí Vell de Lluc splits up from the tarmac road so that one can go on foot, and the tarmac road starts to snake its way up, bend after bend.

Further up one passes next to the **Comuna recreation area** and just afterwards one reaches the Barracar, an old pilgrim's boarding house that today is privately owned. On the right is the large hollow of the **Coma d'en Berruga** and then later we pass the one of Bretxa Nova on whose high part was situated the legendary Grau pass, with the Salt de la Bella Dona. The road has a great deal more bends on its way up and reaches the Coll de la Batalla, a setting-off point for various excursions on foot, such as the well known ascent to the **Puig de Massanella**; it also has a bar/restaurant and a petrol station. From the pass we continue towards **Lluc**, for which we turn right at the Ma-10 road, leaving Escorca and Sóller on the side. For now, we do not consolidate the route on this road that reaches Pollença because at the second intersection, we leave it and turn left on the Ma-2140 road. On the right there is the Can Josep campsite and then we reach the **Sanctuary of Lluc**. We leave the car in the large car park situated on the left of the complex, next to the **Ca s'Amitger recreation area**.

After visiting the sanctuary, a spiritual centre of Mallorca with its image of the Mare de Déu and the church, the pilgrim's square, the museum and the Camí dels Misteris, we redirect our route towards **Pollença**, for which one must retake the short stretch of tarmac that leads us once again to the main Serra road (Ma-10) where one must turn left. We drive through a mountainous area that has oak woods. Towards the 17.4 km point of the road, there is, on the right, the Menut and Binifaldó road, two *possessions* in public ownership. Afterwards there is the **recreation area of Menut**. Further along, on the left, we see the beautiful spot of **Mossa**, with the Puig Caragoler de Femenia and the Puig Roig behind, whilst on the right rise the very high slopes of the Puig Tomir with the property called Muntanya. On the left we pass **Femenia** and **Mortitx**, surrounded by angular rocks worn away by erosion. After Mortitxet, one enters the district of Pollença and the descent starts towards the **Vall d'en Marc**. This is a magnificent valley in which the human and mountain landscapes go hand in hand. The small houses and large houses of the properties run with the Puig Gros de Ternelles on the left and the trio that is made up of the Puig Tomir, the Puig de Ca de Míner and the Cuculla de Fartàritx is on our right. Along land that is already flat, we enter **Pollença** towards the right, next to the Roman

Port de Pollença

bridge. Near to this point, on the left, there is the Ternelles and Castell del Rei road.

After visiting the important historical monuments of Pollença that also has an interesting cultural infrastructure and a great contemporary art tradition as well as a good gastronomic selection, we head towards the **Port de Pollença** (Ma-2200). If there is sufficient time, one should not miss a visit, prior to entering the port, to the **Sant Vicenç cove** (Ma-2203), with its beautiful landscapes, beach, different facilities and archaeological sites. The Port de Pollença merits a stroll alongside the sea in order to contemplate the **bay of Pollença**, between the two arms that close towards the horizon, the one of **Cap de Formentor** and the one of **Cap Pinar**.

From the Port de Pollença we set out on a relatively long route to the **Far de Formentor**, along a winding road (Ma-2210) that leads us for 19 kilometres towards the lighthouse, an authentic Mallorcan *finis terrae*. Near to the Port, on the left, is the area of **Bóquer** and on the right there are some military installations. The road starts to rise near the *possessió* d'Albercutx and links up with, after a few

twists and turns, to landscapes in which the sea is the dominant feature. We will stop at the **Mirador de la Creueta**, where a stepped road leads us to the vertiginously located viewpoint on a precipice that has fascinating views of the **islet Es Colomer,** of Formentor and the mountain range of Cavall Bernat. Once again on the route, the road winds towards the beach of Formentor, with its famous hotel nearby. We continue towards the lighthouse and at the 10.8 km point we come across the *cases velles* (old houses) of Formentor, the centre of a *possessió* rich in history and in the literary reminiscences of the poet **Miquel Costa i Llobera**. Close to the 12.8 km point, we come across the houses of the estate of **Cala Murta**, from where the road sets off to the cove. Further along we pass the Fumat tunnel, a high point that closes, in a natural way, access to the cape. Next, on the left, we can see the landscapes of **Cala Figuera** and Cap de Catalunya. Past the 19 km point and a few kilometres of road further, along the elevated and narrow tongue of land that penetrates the sea, we find ourselves at the **Formentor lighthouse**, one of the most emblematic places of Mallorca.

Next one has to return to the Port de Pollença, where one can choose the options for returning to Palma: one passes through Alcúdia by the Ma-2220 road that has the incentive of following the coast or by the Pollença road (Ma-2200), that passes along the Crestatx area (with its interesting chapel). Another option is to take the Palma-Alcúdia road (Ma-13A) which becomes a motorway (Ma-13) at the point where the second option starts, close to Crestax. By dual carriageway, going southwest, we return towards Palma. Between the towns of Sa Pobla and Inca, we see on the sides of the road the hilltop villages of Búger, on the left, and Campanet, on the right. We leave the town of Inca on the right and, 28 km later we reach Palma, the end of this long route.

Cap de Formentor

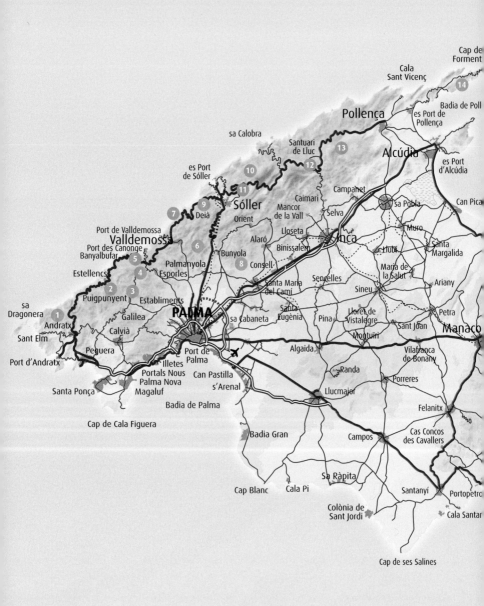

WALKS

⏱ Approximate time (without stops)

🚶 Rating: Difficult   🚶 Rating: Moderate   🚶 Rating: Easy

Majorcan Midwife Toad (*Alytes muletensis*)

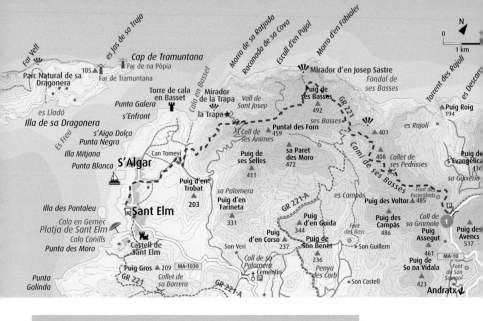

LA TRAPA

Itinerary: Coll de sa Gramola - Es Campàs - Ses Basses - Viewpoint of Cap Fabioler - La Trapa - Can Tomeví - Sant Elm

Ratind: **Medium** | Approximate time (without stops): **3 h 30 m**

We start at the **Coll de la Gramola** (Ma-10 road, Pollença-Andratx, 106 km point). If one comes from Andratx one sees that the road starts a few metres before reaching the kilometre milestone. On the left of the road, we go down a small slope and cross an esplanade: we take the road on the right and then leave the Rajolí road on the right and arrive in the Campàs area where there are remains of formerly cultivated fields. The road remains very uniform, with small and short slopes. Between the Puig des Campàs and Sa Paret des Moros, a view of the **S'Arracó valley** is revealed.

We reach the **Ses Basses** area where there are various houses. The wide road ends at a small, one storey rural house. Behind the house on the same road we are going along, there is a path that goes along a beautiful panoramic route, with the sea on the right and the Puig des ses Basses on the left. At our backs, towards the northeast, there is a spectacular view of the Serra de Tramuntana.

The mountain road, narrow but well streamlined, progresses along a very rugged rocky area with mountain streams that flow towards the sea. At one of the highest points of our route, close to the summit of the Puig de ses Basses, one finds the detour that goes to the **Cap Fabioler viewpoint** (also called that of **Josep Sastre**). It is a small path that goes to the right towards the cliffs. The viewpoint is just over a minute's walk away. It appears to be closed off by a small wall and it affords an extraordinary view of the sea and **Sa Dragonera**.

After visiting the Cap Fabioler viewpoint one needs to retake the same road we are following. Once we have gone back on it there is a short and slight rise in the road; however, it soon starts to descend down the south-western hillside of the Puig de ses Basses. We pass three *rotlos de sitja* (charcoal burner's circles of stones) and the road advances along the north-western hillside of the **Puig de la Trapa**, through the remains of a terrible fire. We can also see what remains of the old terraces that were abandoned long ago.

Shortly after passing a half-demolished side wall, we link up with the wide road that comes from S'Arracó, along the Vall de la Palomera and the Coll de las Ànimes. It is a cart track that descends rapidly towards **La Trapa**.

From La Trapa we set out to go towards **Sant Elm**. At the second bend in the road we are on, a path starts on our right. This first part of the route rises for a short while and there is a good view of the monastery complex. The rise takes us to a natural viewpoint from where we can see, towards the south, the village of Sant Elm and, nearer, **Cala en Basset** with its valley. The descent is very rapid and direct down a slope. It

La Trapa

progresses between rocks and crags and crosses a very uneven stretch that leads to flatter ground between pine trees from which one can see the Torre d'en Basset in more detail and **Sa Dragonera** as a backdrop.

A little further on we again come across a descent with a steep slope that ends in the centre of the valley, where one needs to link up with the road that goes from Sant Elm to Cala en Basset. If one wants to visit the cove, one can reach it in a few minutes: one needs to go to the right in the direction of the descent. The other direction, on the left, is the continuation of the route towards Sant Elm. The road, between pine trees, is wide. We soon arrive at an intersection where the pine grove ends and where there is a house on the left and another on the right, Can Tomeví. We turn in the direction of this house and turn again, this time to the left. We follow the road, that is flat and wide, until we reach a tarmac road of the urbanization that forms part of Sant Elm. After turning left, when the street ends, we reach the town centre. The view of the beach and of the **Pantaleu islet** rounds off our excursion.

Towards Coll de sa Gramola, Cala en Basset and Sa Dragonera

Puig de Galatzó

EL PUIG DE GALATZÓ

Itinerary: Andratx-Estellencs road (Ma-10, Pollença-Andratx, 97 km point) - Shelter of Ses Serveres (SECONA-Son Fortuny) - Pas des Cossi - Pas de na Sabatera - Summit of Puig de Galatzó - Coll del Carnisseret - Spring of Pi - Son Nét Urbanization - Galilea

Rating: **Difficult**　　　　Approximate time (without stops): **3 h 45 m**

Our setting off point is the road that links Andratx to Estellencs at the 97 km point; more specifically, we are between the Grau restaurant and the Coll des Pi. With our back to Andratx, we should follow the wide road to our right in an easterly direction. Near the beginning of the road there is a sign that states that the land we are on is public property. The place is known by the name of Son Fortuny, but it is worth specifying that it should not be confused with the house of the same name from which this land was bought.

We continue going along this cart track for a few minutes with the uneven rocks of the **Penyal des Morro** (653m) standing out over our position. A little further on we reach an important intersection.

The road on the right (southwest) takes one to the Coma d'en Vidal, but we have to follow the road on the left (northeast) towards the Puig de Galatzó, where we continue the walk observing the reddish walls of the left side of the Pas des Cossi. At a little more than five minutes away from the intersection, now on a little slope, we reach the recreation area of **Ses Serveres**. There are tables, benches and a charcoal burner's hut with a rebuilt roof. On the cart track that continues towards the left, that we leave on the side in this itinerary, there is a shelter and there are a few more tables.

Near the hut we take the bridle path that, on its ascent, crosses the **Pas des Cossi**. The path has now been cleaned up and the paving rebuilt. Between pine trees and oak trees we pass an abandoned opening and the path continues towards the right, leaving on the left a small hill on which was the *còssil* (washbowl) that gives the pass its name. We go beyond the stretch that is dominated by oak trees and after a few bends with scattered pine trees, we reach the pass proper, signed by twelve steps that level out the notable unevenness and that lead us to the hillside situated between the Serra dels Pinotells and the Coll de la Moleta Rasa. At the upper part of the pass a T-junction awaits us, with a wooden signpost that indicates the two possible routes: on the left, the **Puig de Galatzó** and on the right, the Mola de l'Esclop. We take the bridle path on the left that will take us to the Puig, with the crags of the Moleta Rasa on the right. We soon reach the Pou de la Sitja, where there is a series of elements relating to the coalman's trade. The area's vegetation includes juniper, hypericum, lentisk and couch grass as well other species.

After the well, the path appears very clear, clean and restored, and there is a short ascent that takes us to the Coll des Morro, a point at which the view is open over Estellencs. Also, the slender outline of the Puig de Galatzó can be clearly seen, with the Mola de Planícia behind. Rosemary and elecampane can be added here to the species of vegetation described before. We pass a paved charcoal stack circle and near a small pine wood, after which we start a light descent that crosses the flow of a stream. We immediately reach a charcoal *ranxo*, with two circles and a hut. Afterwards, in an area with potholes and fissures there starts the ascent towards the **Pas de na Sabatera**. The road has a few bends, often with charcoal stack circles in view. Whilst we ascend, the town of Estellencs becomes more visible. After approximately a quarter of an hour's ascent, among hypericum and rockrose, we link up with the pass that is in a gorge, between crags, and immediately we link up with the road that comes from Estellencs and the houses of the estate of Son Fortuny that goes up to the Puig de Galatzó. Going down towards the left, we would reach Estellencs. We turn right, always in ascent, to reach the summit. After various bends further up, we reach, after a left turn, the place where a small forestry patrol station was located, that now appears abandoned. We are at a crossroads: towards the east, on the left, is the Coll des Carnisseret road, that leads to Puig-punyent and to Galilea and one that we will take later; towards the south, just in front if one is looking at the Puig, there is the road that goes to the summit. It is not very solid and is steep, thus one needs to be as careful as possible.

After the first stretch, there appears the **Mola de l'Esclop**, with its slender, flat and wide summit; the presence of the sea is also more noticeable. Next, we reach the first area to climb. This involves a rocky area that we have to scramble up. Once back on our feet, one passes the mouths of various potholes. Another scramble awaits us, now among rocks that are rather unsteady and that surely became detached from the top during big collapses. After a small raised land area, on the right, we face the last stretch of the ascent, once again along bare rock in the shape of a pass that only separates one from the geodesic apex of the summit by a few metres. The summit of the **Puig de Galatzó** is made up of a magnificent viewpoint, a just award to the effort involved. We go down the same path towards the ruins of the hut. Having reached the crossroads, we turn to the east (on the right, according to the position of descent from the summit), to reach the **Coll des Carnisseret**. The road is a narrow path that advances, with an initial descent, down the rocky hillsides of the Puig de Galatzó. Further on, we pass a heap of loose rocks, small on the first stretch and large on the second part; we undertake the final stretch of the access to the pass. In the mean-time, the first strawberry trees make their appearance, and they intermingle with heather, juniper and lentisk. When we reach the Coll des Carnisseret, the view over Puigpunyent and Galilea opens out before us.

From the pass we follow a road that runs very quickly along the sloping hillside, among dwarf evergreen oaks and strawberry trees. Very soon we enter the oak wood, and with a few turns in descent under the shadows of the wood, we take a pronounced turn to the right and link up with the forest trail on a straight line towards the **Font del Pi**. The spring is close to the beginning of the tarmac, on the left of the road. It has a very run-down appearance, with the remains of a rectangular and generally dry watering hole. At the fork situated by the side of the spring, we follow the left tarmac road where, after another intersection, we turn right; it ends and becomes stony ground that has a descent that ploughs through the stream beds. A little further down we once again take the tarmac and at this point we turn to the left. At the next intersection, we go along the road on the right in descent. We pass near an abandoned quarry and then on the left, we leave on the side various roads that would take us to Puigpunyent.

At about seven minutes away from the quarry, after an opening known by the name of Buzias, there is, on the left, the road of the houses of the estate of Alballutx. Still descending on the tarmac, it takes us about five minutes to reach an important junction of four roads of the **Son Nét** urbanization, with a villa known by the name of "es Cucui". The road on the left goes to Puigpunyent and the road on the right to the Ratxo nature reserve. (Galatzó Reserve)

We follow the road in front of us in a southerly direction that will take us to the high part of **Galilea**. At the next fork we take the road on the right, that is almost a straight line, until the tarmac ends; it forms a roundabout, behind which, slightly to the left, we take the bridle path that penetrates an oak and pine wood. A slight slope allows us to cross a riverbed that, at its highest point, leaves us close to a cart track that ends at the wall of the first villa in Galilea. From the high part of the town, we drop towards the square of the Church, where we end the trip.

Puigpunyent

WALK 3

CAMÍ VELL FROM PUIGPUNYENT TO ESTELLENCS

Itinerary: Puigpunyent - Houses of Son Fortesa - Sa Teulera - Houses of Sa Muntanya - Chapel of Sant Onofre - Coll d'Estellencs - Spring of Son Jover - Son Fortuny (Spring) - Estellencs

Rating: **Moderate**   Approximate time (without stops): **3 h 10 m**

We start the excursion in the village of **Puigpunyent**, in the old Son Bru district, and head in the direction of Esporles (Ma-1101 road). On leaving the village, we turn left onto the Camí Vell (old road) of Estellencs. A metal gate indicates that we are entering the land of the large estate of **Son Fortesa**. The tarmac road, level and comfortable, is soon lined with very tall plane trees and oleanders. On the right we are overlooked by the Puig de na Fàtima, full of legends and tales, whilst on the left there is an expanse of land called Sa Falguera. We pass the torrent of Sa Riera along a small bridge and on the left appears a high wall. The road rises slightly and allows one to observe the large retaining wall that lines the entrance drive to the houses as well as the stepped terraces. The main road turns to the left and goes next to the houses.

Further on, the public road turns to the right, among livestock farms and farm buildings and the tarmac ends. We go through a gate and, on the left, there appear the ruins of a water wheel called Molí de Dalt. The ascent is accentuated and we reach a reservoir. A few minutes later, further up on the left, there is the Creu de l'Ermità (the hermit's cross) and we can continue along an old stretch of bridle path. When we once again link up with the cart track, we find ourselves in front of **Sa Teulera**, a small building with an old tile kiln. Following the road we soon reach the spring of Sa Muntanya, better known as S'Albelló. There is a mine with a lancet arch at half-height to the wall that pours its water into a basin. After a bend on the left we find ourselves near to the houses of the estate of **Sa Muntanya**. Along the main road on the left, there are the ruins of a building called the Carbonera; also on the left, we leave

Sa Teulera

the Coma de Martí Esteve road and follow a new track on the right. We pass an opening and go ahead on the left whilst we enter the oak wood. Further up, in the middle of a maze of new tracks and coalmine paths, we pass an opening called **portell des Bosc** (of the wood) that has a wall on its right. Through strawberry trees and oak trees, we reach the **Sant Onofre chapel** crossroads on the right twelve minutes later. We go down a little through the oak wood to the opening and go along the terraces of the chapel and a small hut. Then we return and pass a threshing floor. From the spring of the chapel, we go up a steep bank and, on the left, we pass a wall. The oak wood leaves us on the cart track of **Sa Campaneta** after passing next to a char-coal stack circle. We take the road on the left, pass next to a large lime kiln and we link up with the Estellencs road at the crossroads

known as Trescollat and we will go up along this road on the right. Seven minutes later and further up, there is the Camí des Puntals on the right and a further five minutes later we reach the **Coll d'Estellencs**.

A large dry stone wall cuts through the Coll d'Estellencs, running along the crest and is aligned to the slope changes. On this wall there is a recently restored opening with a narrow metal gate that has a lock. On the other side of the opening, which is already in the municipal district of Estellencs, the descent starts towards Son Fortuny. The wall is crossed via a *botador* (a jump) of wooden steps on the right of the gate. The pass affords a view of the coast and sea over Estellencs.

We start the descent on the north slope along the oak wood with its strawberry trees, junipers and heather; the remains of the paved path are hardly visible, though some stretches still survive. We leave on the left a path that goes to the high part of the Boal de las Fonts and that links up with the Coll des Carnisseret. On the right there is a large charcoal stack circle and after, the Salt path. On the left we

Houses of Sa Muntanya

pass a track with a large solitary pine tree on the corner. At the next fork we go right as the forest track that we leave continues on the left. After some bends further down, we enter the olive grove and soon after, on the right, we detect a small spring with a water basin tucked away on a slope below a fig tree. Further down we reach the **Font de Son Jover**, which has a rectangular cistern that adapts to the land's unevenness; a large irrigation channel descends from the spring, hidden among the vegetation.

We continue the descent, that combines stretches of old road and new track. Five minutes away from the spring, we leave, on the right, a pylon; in the meantime, there appear before our eyes the houses of the estate of **Son Fortuny**. Continuing our walk, we go towards the left to continue along the old road. We link up with the track after about six or seven minutes.

Very soon we take the road on the right that leads us to the spring of **L'Ull de s'Aigua**. The jet of water springs up from the bowels of the earth and oak trees, poplars, brambles and bushes always shadow and keep the place cool. Near to the spring we cross the torrent and follow the bridle path that crosses a small gate and goes along between small walls. The houses of the estate of Son Fortuny are further up. We pass a second gate and just after we link up with the cart track that we just broach as we can take a short cut that leaves us on a bend below the road. Just after, we pass along a bridge over the torrent and then arrive at the Volta de s'Arraval, with its recently built cistern. After other bends further down, amongolive trees, is the final part of the excursion. After passing through a metal gate, we are soon in Estellencs, near to the public wash house and the town square.

Xiprell (*Erica multiflora*)   Estepa joana (*Hypericum balearicum*)

Camí Vell del Correu, on the way to Coll del Pi

CAMÍ VELL DEL CORREU
FROM ESPORLES TO BANYALBUFAR

Itinerary: Esporles - Pont de la Turbina (Ma-1100, km 2.2) - El Garrover Cremat - La Potada del Cavall (Portell de Son Valentí) - Coll des Pi - Son Sanutges (plaster works) - Font de la Vila - Banyalbufar

Rating: **Easy**	Approximate time (without stops): **2 h 30 m**

The **Camí Vell del Correu** is an authentic royal road, medieval in origin and already documented in the 15th century; it starts at Esporles, next to the parish church of Sant Pere, and goes uphill on Sant Pere, with the church on our right. Continuing our walk, we reach the opening of Bellavista on the left and the last houses of the town on the right. Now the road continues as a dirt track, similar to a bridle path.

A sign indicates that the road has been restored and another tells us that **Banyalbufar** is about two hours away on foot. The road progresses between small stone walls and takes us to a high level where there are cultivated fields that extend towards the right and a bank that rises on the left. Just eight or nine minutes from the open-

ing of Bellavista, we reach a small gate. At this point the descent starts towards the road. Very soon we see the beautiful image that is made up of a proud collection of plane trees (*Platanus orientalis*) that are already on Comuna land. We reach the tarmac road that we have approached rapidly, after having left a covered reservoir to the right and having passed another wooden gate.

We cross the Esporles-Banyalbufar (Ma-1100) road. The footpath, which has been restored according to traditional dry stone techniques, continues at the other side. We go beyond a new stone ramp and walk along a stretch with plane trees and the road on the left until we reach the bridge known as **de la Turbina**, that formed part of the 19th-century road. The bridge crosses the torrent of Sant Pere or Esporles, that from here is on our left and that is surrounded by a lot of vegetation (oak trees, poplars, wild olives, a few fig trees, ivy, wild peach trees and the very tall ash trees as well as other species).

Further ahead, on the left, there is the **Camí del molí Draper**. We then pass near the Puigpunyent crossroads (Ma-1101) intersection which also goes to La Granja. From a little further on from the Granja intersection (the 1.5 km point of the Ma-1100 road), we continue walking for about two hundred metres along the rebuilt road towards Banyalbufar. We pass the cart track of the **Es Murtar** property that converges onto the road just on our left, near to the 2 hectometre point (1.2 km point). At this point, called the **Garrover Cremat**, we cross the road and ascend a paved ramp, after which, slightly to our right, we link up once again with the old Correu road. After a few minutes we reach an opening that separates the municipal districts of Esporles and Banyalbufar; a little further on there is the not very clear fork, where we have to take the upper road on our left. The road soon continues behind a dry stone wall with an opening that allows one to cross the oak wood.

After the opening, the road, that is not very defined, continues towards the right. We see a lime kiln and a hut on the left. A dry stone wall appears on the right side of the road and further on we link up with the road that connects with the houses of the estate of Ses Mosqueres, that rises on the right, with an opening with a metal gate.

We enter a pine wood that has a dry stone wall on the right. We pass another fork and we take the left road that has an uneven surface and goes through oak trees and strawberry trees. From this moment the road follows an ascending course with several bends. After a solitary step, there is a small hole in the middle of the road known as **Sa Potada des Cavall** (the kick of a horse). On the left we can see a charcoal stack circle and a hut, and very soon we pass by a watercourse. Further on we see the sea in the distance over the Port des Canonge area; a new track is already near and it crosses our road. On the right of the track there is the so called **Era des Moro**, a privileged spot with good views. About two minutes later we reach a large lime kiln that has very thick walls. Carrying on, we pass a landslip of the road. Some specimens of juniper trees are incorporated in the vegetation of the area. On the right side there is a notable wall of large rocks. If we look up, we see the sea towards Sa Foradada and the *possessió* of Son Bunyola. The road goes along the **Coll des Pi** (453m) that is situated between the Puig de s'Argenter on the right and the Puig de sa Barca on the left.

The descent of the saddle is on stony ground, with a ruined wall on the right; strawberry trees, heather and brambles invade the road. We next reach the boundary of **Son Creus**, with a dry stone wall that closes off the road transversally. There is a jump of wooden steps to climb over the wall in order to continue; on the other side, we proceed over the fallen leaves of oak trees, and there is a high wall on the left and a small wall on the right. A few metres further on, we reach another wall that closes off the road. After passing over to the other side, we go towards the right where the Correu road continues. In this way, we reach the intersection of the Font des Garbell or Planícia road. At this important crossroads, we see that to the left there is a road that leads to Son Sanutges, S'Arboçar and Planícia, and a branch of which reaches the Font des Garbell. Towards the right, this same road descends towards the Ma-10 road. At said point, just on the left, there are the remains of what was the gypsum kiln of **Son Sanutges**.

The Camí del Correu, with a layer of tarmac from here, continues to descend on a steep slope towards Banyalbufar. On the right, one can see the houses of the estate of **Son Creus**. Whilst we descend, we can contemplate the big impact caused by the quarry. Further on, we pass next to a hut and a threshing floor; the view over Banyalbufar becomes bigger and bigger. We link up, on the left, with the canal that comes from the **Vila spring**; it flows very close to the Torrent d'en Roig, that occupies the central part of the Comellar des Llims and falls into the sea. Meanwhile, at the low part, one can see a group of three reservoirs that form part of the water complex close to the spring.

After the Font de la Vila and the reservoirs, with large oaks on the right, we leave on the left the road that goes up to the houses of the estate of S'Arboçar. More houses and other smaller *safareigs* (open water tanks) continue to appear. Further down, Es Verdaguer and Son Albertí are on the left, followed by a road that runs next to the large *safareig* of **Son Vives** that links up with the village of **Es Penyal**, on the outskirts of Banyalbufar. We leave on the right the house of Sa Plana that has been extensively altered, and continue around a small bend, the so-called **Es Porxo**; then we pass, still down a marked descent, in front of the houses of the estate of Son Borguny that are already in the town centre. Going along Jeroni Alberti street, we enter Banyalbufar square.

Safareig of Son Albertí (Banyalbufar)

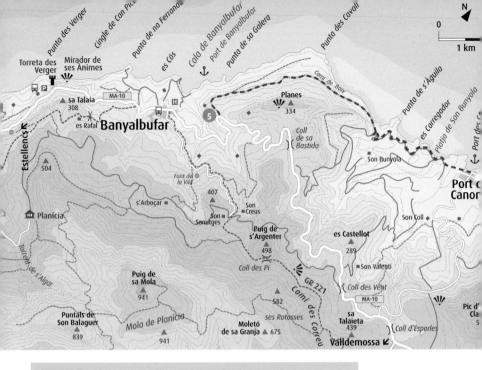

LA VOLTA DEL GENERAL AND CAMÍ DE BAIX DE SON BUNYOLA

Itinerary: the Ma-10 road (Pollença-Andratx) 82.250 km point - Port des Canonge - The Ma-10 road 82.250 km point

Rating: **Easy**   Approximate time (without stops): **2 h 20 m**

Our setting off point is the 85.250 km point on the Ma-10 road (Pollença-Andratx), prior to reaching Banyalbufar if we come from Palma, on a bend that forms a small esplanade. We start the route along a road called **Volta des General**, a name that refers to General Ferran Cotoner, the landlord of the Baronia de Banyalbufar who, at the end of the 19th century, contributed to the repairs of the main road. In olden days, this road was called Camí de Baix de Son Bunyola.

Just at the start, the road turns to the right and runs parallel to the sea during all its journey. About three minutes after leaving the road, there is a restored villa on our left called La Cabarola. The enclave affords a magnificent view over the village of Banyalbufar, with the mountain called the Mola de Planícia as a backdrop.

Very soon we pass next to a modern cistern and we continue along the wide road, down a slight slope, until we reach the access gate of the **Son Bunyola** property. We ignore the road that comes from the left, from Pla des Cavall, and go up a slight ascent. On the right there is the Puig de ses Planes (334m) and, towards the sea, the Punta des Cavall.

Without difficulty, we reach the ruins of old buildings at the place called Sa Caseta d'en Pere Antoni. From Sa Caseta the road is flat and the sea is always on the left. Strawberry trees, heather, shrubs, juniper trees, couch grass, a few wild carob trees and a few oak trees

Port des Canonge

are present with the pine trees. The road is adorned with protective stones lined up on the left. Further along, we pass close to a lime kiln on the right.

In the meantime, our route goes along a flat ledge, with crags of the northeast spur of the **Puig de Ses Planes**, called Es Revellar on our right. The area is known as **Es Corral Fals**. The cut down crags that rise on the right are a conglomerate often stuck on the road, as though they were cut to make the road possible. We continue in descent and reach a three road intersection, where we take the road on the left. After a bend, we leave on the right the road that goes directly to the houses of the estate of Son Bunyola. We continue, heading to the left, until we approach **Punta de l'Àguila**, a crag that rises erect over the sea. In the environs, an outcrop of reddish rocks stands out. These are the well known *pedres d'esmolar* (whetstones). We leave behind on the coastline the beach of Carregador and the Ses Garroves jetty, used traditionally for the shipping of agricultural products.

At the next intersection we go towards the left, close to the sea according to the path, and we pass a second road, on the right, after which there is a small high plateau situated close to the beach of Son Bunyola, covered in pine trees and the remains of a building called Es Vestidors. Along a path between shrubs, we can follow the steps that separate us from the beach. The torrent of Son Bunyola flows into the beach that has two dry docks on its right. We leave the beach on the slope that is close to the dry docks. The path we are now taking goes along parallel to the sea, between shrubs. Soon we reach the area called Cala Gata, with the ruins of a building that used to house a tile workshop. After passing the bed of the Son Coll torrent, that flows a few metres ahead, a large esplanade awaits us called **Tanca de la Mar** (the enclosure of the sea). We cross it and on the other side we come across the houses of **Port des Canonge**.

From the Port des Canonge we return towards the Son Bunyola beach and approach the **Camí de Baix de Son Bunyola** that, via Corral Fals, will take us once again to the Volta des General and the road where this itinerary ends.

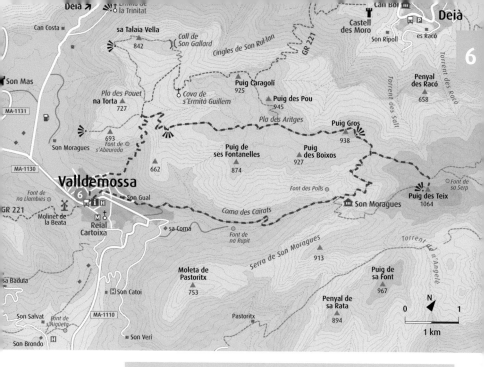

WALK 6

EL PUIG DES TEIX

ALONG PLA DES POUET AND COMA DELS CAIRATS

Itinerary: Valldemossa - Font de s'Abeurada - Pla des Pouet gate - Pas d'en Miquel - Pla des Aritges - Pla de sa Serp - Summit of Puig des Teix - Casa de neu (ice house) of Son Moragues - Font des Polls - Font de na Rupit - Houses of the estate of Son Gual - Valldemossa

| Rating: **Difficult** | Approximate time (without stops): **3 h 55 m** |

We start the excursion next to the state school of Valldemossa. One needs to climb a set of steps on the left that will take us to some urban streets that seem like a small maze. We firstly turn right and then left; once again left and lastly right, where finally we come to the beginning of the cart track that is not tarmacked. On the right, behind a barbed-wire fence, a new track begins that leads to Son Gual. After a bend to the left the path opens up to the oak wood. We immediately find the diversion for **Ses Basses**, along the road on the right and nearby there is a metal gate with a jump of wooden steps that we need to go over: on the other side, with a slight turning to the left, we continue along the road that is now accompanied by a small canal on its left side. A little further on, just a few metres on the left from the first bend, we reach the spring of **S'Abeurada**. It is situated in a coalmining zone.

We go back a few metres from where we came to return on the **Pla des Pouet** road. There then starts a steep rise that has many twists and turns in order to cope with the great unevenness; very soon it places the town of Valldemossa at our feet. It is possible to use a few short cuts that go from the road to our right and that, in reality, are the remains of an old paved road. Having reached the Pla de Pouet gate, we realise that this is an appropriate spot in which to catch our breath.

By going north, in a straight line according to our position, we can reach Pla des Pouet in a short time. However, our route follows the road on the right, initially in parallel with the wall that comes from the gate. Not very far away, the road crosses a considerable unevenness with a few bends supported by a large side bank. This spot is known by the name of **Pas d'en Miquel**. Having crossed the pass, we enter the lands of the public property of **Son Moragues**; a wooden sign reminds us of this.

A little further, on the right, we come across two viewpoints that afford views of Valldemossa and the surrounding areas. From the main road one reaches, through a short paved diversion on the right, the first viewpoint, situated in a place called **La Regata de les Onze**. Just a few metres from this viewpoint, on the right once one has returned to the road, there was an area of charcoal stack circles whose name has been preserved: **Ranxo d'en Sutró**. To reach the second viewpoint (known as **Mirador de ses Basses**) we need to make a detour from the main road, about ten metres on the right. We will return to it in order to continue going through the oak wood. After about fifteen minutes of leaving the Mirador de ses Basses, we stop to see the **Ses Fontanelles** water tank that is on the left of the road at a few metres distance.

From the water tank we return to the road that then goes through a more deforested area where already there are no oak trees. The Puig dels Boixos (874m) appears on the right. Soon we see a ring of pine trees that indicate to us the position of the place called the **Pla des Aritges**. Close to the pine trees we link up with the **Camí de l'Arxiduc**, that is on our left; this road goes to Puig Caragolí. We follow towards the right in order to promptly reach the zone of the **Cova de l'Aigua** (the water cave). To reach it, we leave the road on the right at a point where there are a few pine trees. The cave is small and flooded by the action of a meagre trickle of water that occurs at the bottom of the cavity. We continue on the Camí de l'Arxiduc, that runs along the high cliff that rises above the north coast. In all of this area we can enjoy an unsurpassed panoramic view over the surrounding areas of **Deià**. After a few minutes, one needs to look out for a fork in the road as we have to leave the Camí de l'Arxiduc, that takes one to the Coma dels Cairats, and turn left and follow the ascent towards the Puig des Teix. This intersection is close to the place known as **Racó Perdut** (the lost corner).

The snowy summit of Puig des Teix

The new road is narrower than the Arxiduc one; very soon we cross an uneven patch in the form of a step that needs a simple climb. Soon we reach a wall that marks the end of the public property of Son Moragues. We need to climb over the wall at its left end, close to an uneven patch in which there are old livestock enclosures. To get down off the wall, there is a wooden step called a *botador*. Once we have negotiated the wall, we are practically already in the **Pla de sa Serp**, a spacious esplanade that constitutes the last natural step prior to reaching the summit of the **Puig des Teix**, whose mound appears gigantically to our right. From the Pla de sa Serp (the plain of the snake) we start to take on the final ascent, for which we go up along the small dirt and stone path to the narrow pass between the Teixot (1,063m) on our left and the summit of the Puig des Teix (1,064m). From the pass we head towards the right, and aim directly for the highest point of the summit. Rockroses and the *coixinets de monja* ("nun's cushions", endemics that adopt rounded shapes by the action of the wind) will be the only vegetation to accompany us. In a few minutes we reach the summit, where we find a geodesic landmark. The panoramic view will be a good reward for the effort one has made, nothing less than the conquest of one of the most characteristic heights of the Mallorcan mountains.

We descend by the same route we took for the ascent, towards the Pla de sa Serp. Just before reaching it, we make a slight detour to the right (NE), to visit the Font de sa Serp, from where we retake the road that links up with that of l'Arxiduc; we pass again the *botador* of the Corral dels Bous wall, we go down the rocky step and join the Camí de l'Arxiduc at the intersection that, on the left, puts us in the direction of the **Coma des Cairats**. After the Racó Perdut, the descent starts along a paved road with tight bends and in the meantime, the oak trees reappear.

After passing a wider stretch with loose stones, one reaches the *casa de neu* of **Son Moragues**. Further down there is a shelter that was the old house of the *nevaters* (the snow-collectors, ice-makers). Nearby starts the forest track that has a steep slope descent. After a bend on the left, we leave a pond on the right and the track outlines

6

more bends up to the **Font dels Polls** where there are wooden tables and benches for meals.

On our path, the slope becomes more noticeable, with bends that are very marked by the unevenness that we are crossing and in the meantime, charcoal stack circles and lime kilns on the sides of the road appear. We thus reach the first example of a traditional activity: the *ranxo* of the charcoal maker. The track descends now without bends and there are many charcoal stack circles on the area. Further down, on the right, there appears the second popular mountain culture element that has been saved along this watercourse. It is a lime kiln whose oven has been restored and it is an example of lime production starting from the firing of lime rocks.

Soon we reach the end boundary of the Son Moragues property, where there is a signpost on the right of the Conselleria d'Agricultura i Pesca del Govern les Illes Balears, followed by a pass with a wooden gate that needs to be negotiated by the stone step *botador* on the left. From here we continue along the cart track towards the southwest, among the first olive trees. A first turn on the right, followed by another to the left, leaves us next to the **Font de na Rupit**, that is in a ruinous state. We continue in order to reach, after a couple of minutes, an intersection. On the left, the road of the houses of Sa Coma continues. On the right, the Valldemossa road continues, after an opening with a grate that prevents livestock from crossing it; we continue with our nearly completed itinerary along this last road.

After crossing an opening that has no gate, the road has a bend towards the left; we leave another opening on our right which is of bricks and has a metal gate. We thus reach the urbanization of Arxiduc which means the end of the cart track and the beginning of the asphalted Carrer Toscana. We leave behind a carob tree that occupies the centre of the asphalt and enter Carrer Lluis Vives, where there are various residential villas, and reach the beautiful 16th-century defence tower of the houses of the estate of **Son Gual**. From here, we cross the Palma to Deià road and enter the town of Valldemossa, where our excursion ends.

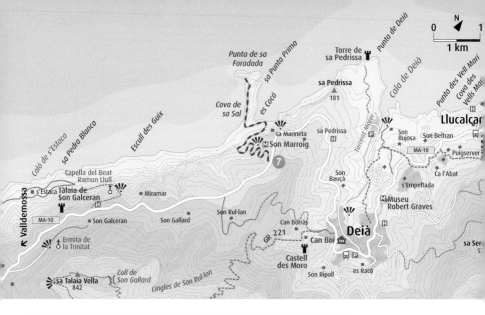

SA FORADADA

SON MARROIG

Itinerary: Son Marroig (Valldemossa-Deià road, Ma-10) - Viewpoint of Rotlo Gros - Sa Foradada - Houses of the state of Son Marroig

Rating: **Easy**	Approximate time (without stops): **1 h 40 m**

The houses of the estate of Son Marroig are on the Valldemossa to Deià road (Ma-10, Pollença-Andratx), at km 65.6. The road goes down to the **Son Marroig viewpoint** (Galliner viewpoint), with a spectacular view over Sa Foradada. On the left are the houses, with a 16th-century defence tower and the collections of the house/museum of the Archduke Ludwig Salvator. We leave the houses and the water tank on our right and come across a metal gate, surrounded by plane trees with a *botador* to negotiate to the other side. On this stretch of the road, remains of tarmac are visible. Soon there is a turning to the right. Close to a gate in the wall we can observe the outline of the Son Marroig viewpoint that is in the form of a small Ionic temple. On the other side is an olive tree plantation where the Camí des Barranc starts. Next, we leave on our left a road that leads to a villa. A few metres further we reach the **Sa Foradada viewpoint** that is situated on the right of the road, among spurges and lentisk.

The viewpoint has this name because from here one can contemplate the exceptional rocky spur. A wall protects the north side, from where there is the best view; in the middle of the small enclosure, there is a sculpted stone table that was placed over an old olive trunk.

From the Sa Foradada viewpoint, the road descends more steeply, with a bend on the right and another on the left. We reach the base of a precipice with karst concretions that rise on our right. Next we pass a gully with a paved ford, something that repeats itself at the bends on the descent. We continue the descent until we reach the **Rotlo Gros** (the large circle) viewpoint. This viewpoint was built on a crag that became isolated when the Sa Foradada road was built. One reaches it up a flight of steps that leads to the summit of the crag, where there is a small circular shaped esplanade that gave the viewpoint its name. It is surrounded by a protective wall.

Sa Foradada

Going down towards the viewpoint, we go round three more bends and pass a paved ford in which the effects of landslides are visible. After the next bend, we reach the **Coll de sa Foradada**. This point is an intersection as the **Camí de la Mar** that links up with Es Guix, goes to the left, whilst the Camí de Sa Foradada goes to the right, near Cala des Cocó. Walking for the moment along Camí de la Mar, it is evident that it was an important road that reached **S'Estaca**.

From the pass of Sa Foradada, we go to the end of the peninsula along a flat road with an attractive view. The sea is on the right, separated from the road by a protective wall, whilst the rest of the Sa Foradada isthmus is on the left, with naturally sculpted borehole rocks. At six or seven minutes away from the first pass, we turn left where there is a small spur on the right called Punta Prima; if we look at this side towards the northeast, we see how the coastline stretches towards the Gros de Sóller cape. After the bend in the road, we head to the nearby second pass of Sa Foradada, where we see on the left some buildings used as a restaurant in summer. If we look towards the famous crag, on the right is Caló de la Punta Prima, whilst on the left, bordered by the Morro de Sa Foradada, is the Racó de Sa Foradada, a small cove with the remains of a small jetty that was in use during the Archduke's time.

One can go up to the highest point of **Sa Foradada** within about ten minutes, via a difficult and dangerous pass that includes a few climbs. This pass leaves us at a narrow pass, on whose left we link up with the upper vertex, that has a cube-shaped boundary stone that was installed by the crew of the Vulcano steamship on the occasion of the triangulation in 1893.

From the top, we return back along the same road, firstly along the pass near the rock and then along the Sa Foradada road where the ascent proper starts. We pass the Rotlo Gros viewpoint and, going up, we link up once again with the Sa Foradada viewpoint from where, very soon, we reach the metal gate that leaves us once more at the houses of the estate of **Son Marroig**, where the excursion ends.

Rocky formations in Sa Foradada and Port de S'Estaca

Avenc de Son Pou

COANEGRA AND AVENC OF SON POU

Itinerary: Quatre Cantons (Santa Maria) - Houses of Son Torella - Houses of Son Oliver - Houses of Son Roig - Houses of Son Pou - Avenc of Son Pou - Torrent des Freu - Houses of Es Freu - Bunyola/Orient road (Ma-2100), km 8.3

Rating: **Moderate**   Approximate time (without stops): **3 h**

We set off at the **Quatre Cantons** (four corners), an intersection where the Coanegra and Raiguer roads cross. We go along the Coanegra road and a little further, we pass the Camí de s'Arboçar that is on the right. We continue along tarmac, between small stone walls, and leave the Camí de na Cili on the left and, the Cals Frares and Son Verdera zones on the right. On the left of the road we see the high houses of the estate of Son Fortesa. Just a little further on, a short distance from the road, there appears on our left the country house of **Son Torrella**.

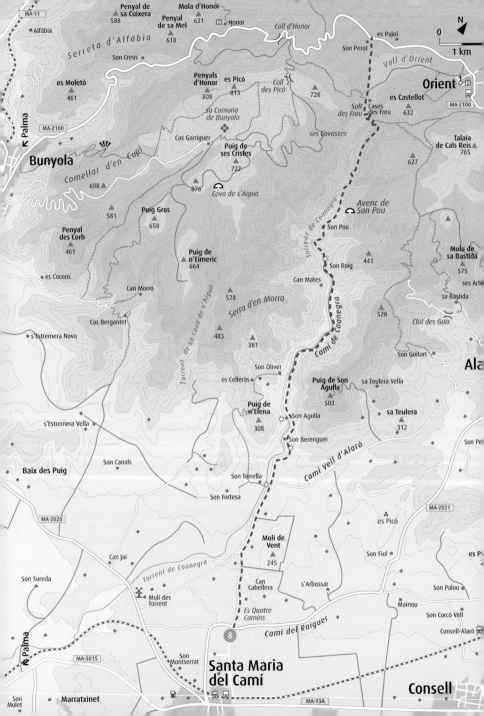

Along the Coanegra road, after Son Torrella, we leave the old Santa Maria road to Alaró on the right, and pass the houses of the estate of Son Palou. Further along, on the left, and behind a fence, one comes across the first aqueduct of the Coanegra stream, called Son Palou. In the meantime, the road penetrates the deep **Coanegra valley**. In the orographic panorama, the Puig de Son Gulla and the Puig de Son Guitard, on the right, stand out, as do the eastern foothills of the Comuna de Bunyola on the left. Later we reach the houses of the estate of Son Berenguer.

Less than five minutes later, Son Gulla appears, situated below the crags of the peak of the same name. Prior to linking up with the opening of the houses of the estate of **Son Oliver**, a metal gate closes the pass to vehicles. About two minutes after having passed it, we come across the said opening and the houses, situated on the left of the road, just after, the tarmac ends. Whilst we are walking along the plain area, the Coanegra torrent accompanies us on the left, with its pine trees and a few fig trees. At some ten or twelve minutes from the houses, we can see the Coanegra ditch that flows above the torrent along a one-arched aqueduct. We cross the torrent via a paved ford and both the torrent and the watercourse from here are on our right, below a vertically cut crag. The ruins of the Bassa de Cas Barreter are also on the right of the route, half hidden in the vegetation. Next, very soon, a charcoal stack circle appears on the left with oak trees and pine trees around it; the Can Mates house can be seen above the steep bank.

Fruit trees announce that we are close to the houses of the estate of **Son Roig**, that we reach just after crossing a bridge over the torrent.

Further on, with the torrent to our left, we pass a metal gate and see the small house of Can Millo. A little while after passing the orange tree plantations on the left, we reach the houses of the estate of **Can Morei**.

Before, on the right, there are some hollows in the natural wall, used to shelter livestock. At three minutes from Can Morei we reach the houses of the estate of Son Pou. If one cannot pass through the houses, one must go up the detour on the right, which returns to the path.

Just a little over one hundred metres and on the right of the road, below some rocky peaked crags with a grotto with calcareous concretions, is the Coanegra spring, known also by the name of **S'Ullal de Son Pou**. We can see the mouth of a circular well, usually closed by a metal lid; it is a ventilation well of the *qanat* or canal where the water runs from the spring. After the Coanegra spring the road is flat and leaves on its left a group of olive trees, after which the torrent is once again near. Soon we reach an esplanade dominated by a lime kiln that is on the right. At this point, the cart track turns into a bridle path, typical in the mountains, in the direction of Freu and Orient. The first part of this bridle path is uphill and leads us to the **pothole of Son Pou**. At about seven or eight minutes from the lime kiln, we reach an intersection. If one wishes to visit the **avenc**, one abandons the main road that goes on to Orient and takes the detour to the right.

The pothole road goes rapidly along a short uneven stretch with nine relatively short bends and at just ten minutes from the Camí d'Orient. Finally we reach a small esplanade where we find an artificial gallery that penetrates the interior of the pothole. This is a very curious cavity, surprising for its size. It forms a spacious rotunda of some 150 metres long by 70 metres wide approximately. It occupies the interior of a hollow mound, that has on its highest part, at some seventy metres from the ground, an orifice that is the only natural entrance, with a mouth of some ten metres high by eight metres wide. It is interesting to observe the light effect produced by the sun's rays when they penetrate this entrance. There are also stalactites and stalagmites.

At the lowest part, to the left, there is another chamber in which the limited light from the large chamber fades. However, one can hear the drips of water that fall in a pond and note the irregularities of the floor, with dense *gours*, formations of karst erosion that form pitted textures and contain small quantities of embalmed water.

On the right of the entrance to the pothole there is another chamber, smaller but with more examples of calcareous filigree, that can be accessed by an artificial staircase. The gallery or passageway, that is the actual entrance, was made in 1894.

After having visited the pothole, we return to descend the same road until we link up with the main road, that we follow to the right, in the direction of Orient. After just five minutes, we are in front of

Camí de Coanegra and charcoal-burner's hut

Ses Covasses, that is located on the other side of the torrent's basin, on our left. At this point we need to pay careful attention because the natural tendency would be to continue slightly towards the right, in a north-easterly direction, but this would take us along the Comellar dels Bous, outside our itinerary. Meanwhile, in front of Ses Covasses, we take the left lane, momentarily in the direction of the torrent, then we soon get back to a northerly course. The road is narrow now and the vegetation dense. A little further along, with a retaining wall, the lane becomes wider, and soon we reach an intersection. We go along the most defined road, slightly towards the right, and after two uphill bends, we ignore a short cut on the right and continue along the wide road. Halfway along the road there appears a charcoal stack circle and a hut on the left. Strawberry trees and oak trees dominate the vegetation, with juniper trees, buckthorn, heather and grey leaved cistus. We leave another short cut on the right and go round a double bend to reach, a few minutes later, a lime kiln and, immediately after, a very wide charcoal stack circle.

After passing this circle, there is an important fork: our route follows the road on the left (the road on the right takes one towards Orient along the Pas de l'Estaló). Soon we reach an opening in the dry stone wall, after which there is a bend to the right that affords a panoramic view over the houses of the estate of Freu and part of the Vall d'Orient, with the Serra d'Alfàbia in the background. The road now appears wide and solid, in descent towards the crossroads that exist before crossing the **Freu torrent**; on the left is the Salt des Freu area. Along this short optional road, we will see the ruins of an old water mill on the other side of the bank, and the different levels of the torrent. If we are lucky and there is water, the spectacle is guaranteed.

Once again at the junction of the Camí de Son Pou and the Torrent des Freu, we cross the riverbed that is really divided into two courses. At about twenty metres to the north, we come across a metal gate with metal steps against it to cross it. Once we have negotiated the gate, we immediately reach the ruined **houses of the estate of Freu**. We go back on the final part of the road that is wide and flat. After a short distance, we come across the Font des Freu on our left. From here, the road continues, between plantations and stone walls. We leave behind two reservoirs on the right, next to a ring of tall pine trees. In the meantime, we will see the **Orient valley** that opens itself up spectacularly to the northeast, flanked by a barrier of mountains that stretch from the Serra d'Alfàbia to Ofre and the Serra de la Rateta.

Orient valley

It does not take us long to enter once again an oak wood environment, where we come across a metal gate with a wooden step to negotiate. About a hundred metres further ahead appears the Ma-2100 road (Bunyola-Alaró), at approximately the 8.3 km point. Orient is on our right at a distance of about one and a half kilometres.

The Freu torrent

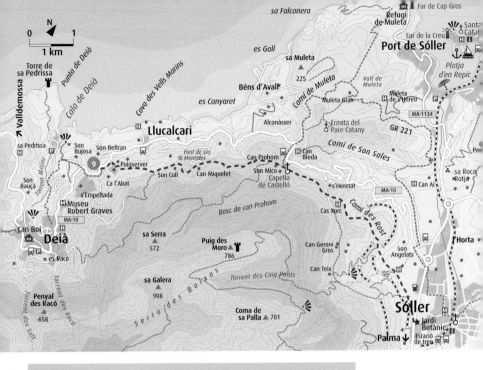

WALK 9

CAMÍ DE CASTELLÓ AND CAMÍ DEL ROST

FROM DEIÀ TO SÓLLER

Itinerary: The Deià-Sóller road 60. km point (Ma-10 Pollença-Andratx) - Houses of the estate of Son Coll - Can Miquelet - Houses of Son Mico and Can Prohom - Chapel of Castelló - L'Heretat - Sóller

Rating: **Easy**	Approximate time (without stops): **2 h 15 m**

The **Camí de Castelló** is a road with medieval origins, and it was the central artery road of the old communication link of Deià and Sóller with the flat part of the island, starting from the Coll de Sóller. A branch of the main road, namely the stretch that goes from S'Heretat to Sóller, is known as **Camí del Rost** (of the slope), a name that perfectly illustrates the unevenness that covers this area with the slopes of Son Angelats. Both on the Castelló road and the Rost road, one notices the refurbishment and restoration work carried out by the **Escola de Margers**, where techniques and applications of dry stone walling are taught. This is an age-old craft that is integral to the mountainous landscape.

The excursion starts at the 60.25 km point of the Ma-10 road, just after passing the road that goes from Cal Abat to Deià. Between the houses that the road borders, there starts a stepped road that very soon turns to the left and is eaten up by a tarmac road that goes on between new villas. After walking for about two minutes, we leave the tarmac because the old road reappears on our left, marking a north/northeast direction and on a slight ascent amongst pine trees and olive trees. Soon we are surrounded by a good view of the environs of Llucalcari, that stretches out towards Sa Pedrissa and Es Còdols Blancs, close to Cala de Deià. We leave on the right a large ivy covered rock with a small cave at its base; in the meantime, we approach directly over **Llucalcari**. Three minutes later, we see that on the right there is a track that goes up to the house called Can Toni Boi. Five or six minutes later, we reach the houses of the estate of Son Coll; they were put up in a *possessió* that has its origins in the 13th century, as a recent tile indicates. Renovated over time, the houses are currently divided into distinct properties. In this stretch that surrounds **Son Coll**, the road continues, tightly fitting in between the paraments of the houses, on the right, and a stone wall on the left.

Camí del Rost

From Son Coll to **Can Miquelet** the road descends in steps. Shortly before the houses of the estate of Can Miquelet, there is a detour on the left with a short stepped descent, next to the vehicular road that takes us to the Font de Ses Mentides (spring of lies), also called **Font de Son Coll**. The source appears in a small corner, with a stone bench and a small spring with a conduit and a rectangular basin.

From the spring, we return to the Camí de Castelló, that crosses the tarmac track and continues paved in front of Can Miquelet. We go slightly uphill and are surrounded by pine trees and oak trees; after about seven minutes, we pass a small wooden gate and we catch a glimpse of some charcoal stack circles. We cross a watercourse between shady oak trees and, keeping slightly to the left, with irregular crags on our right, we reach a stepped slope that is negotiated round four bends and is the highest pass of the excursion. A brief stop to contemplate the landscape allows us to see the **Casa Nova** on the left, with its fortified tower. A little further on, a gate opens up to the **Can Prohom** olive grove, next to the wall with tumbledown stretches. Before the houses of the estate of **Son Mico**, there is a good example of a threshing floor that has a steep face to avoid the slope of the ground. Towards the northeast, one sees the so called S'Ensaïmada pine tree and, further away, the Puig Major. We soon come to an interesting set of two possessió houses, that appear to be joined: on the right, the the houses of Son Mico, and on the left those of Can Prohom.

Camí de Castelló

Going down a section of paved road, about a hundred metres from Can Prohom, we find the recently restored 17th-century **chapel of Castelló**. Close to the chapel are the houses of the estate of **Can Carabasseta**; on the right of the road and a little further, on the left, are those of **S'Heretat**. Here, there is an important intersection: to the left there is the road that leads to the Deià-Sóller road, whilst our route heads more to the right, on a descent, along a road that is now wider and runs between olive trees, with a few olive-picker sheds in view. This is the Camí del Rost, that goes directly to Sóller. In this area one easily finds gypsum stones that gave rise to the craft activity of converting the gypsum for use in building.

Further on, we border the bed of the watercourse that flows deeply on our left and just after a new metal gate, from where there

are views of the Torre Picada in the background, the pass becomes narrower and continues towards the left; we ignore the wider road on the right that comes to a halt in front of a gate. Soon our route becomes wider, after going through a small wooden gate and we once again go along a paved flight of steps, now remarkably wide and interrupted by a stretch of tarmac. The descent becomes more pronounced, forming twists and turns and a little further down, we pass near the Sóller railway line, above one of the rail tunnels. Myrtle characterizes the area's vegetation. On the right we can observe the bridge the train passes over and, next to the road, a small fountain with a water collection pipe. After passing the **Cinc Ponts** (five bridges) **torrent**, we reach a metal gate on the left that, in days gone by, was the access to the gardens of Son Angelats.

The paved road ends at the Mont-reals opening, with stone abutments, and we leave this on the right. A few metres further, and already in the area known by the name of **Pla d'en Bieleta**, the tarmac reappears on the road and one can see the first houses on the outskirts of the city. After Vila Frontera, on the left, we leave the **Can Puig** building on the right, that used to house an electricity "factory", and reach the main road that, towards the left, goes to the Port de Sóller, just in front of the petrol station. A monolith on the right literally indicates : "Deià a peu. Camí del Rost 7.93 km" (Deià on foot. Camí del Rost 7.93 km). We can reach the centre of Sóller, after having crossed the road, via the road that runs on the right of the service station.

Panorama of Sa Costera

WALK 10

FROM MIRADOR DE SES BARQUES TO TUENT BY SA COSTERA

Itinerary: Viewpoint of ses Barques - Bàlitx d'Amunt - Bàlitx d'Enmig - Bàlitx d'Avall - Coll de Biniamar - Sa Costera - Font des Verger (Electricity "factory") - Capapuig - Cala Tuent

Rating: **Moderate**   Approximate time (without stops): **4 h**

We begin the excursion at the **Mirador de Ses Barques**, next to the Sóller to Lluc (Ma-10) road at the 44.9 km point. In front of the same viewpoint, towards the north, a road starts that leads to the three properties called **Bàlitx**. It is a wide road, suitable for vehicles. However, for walkers it is recommended to take the bridle path that is initially paved and just on the right of the cart track. After a short ascent, we descend to return to the *possessió* road of the Bálitx, just before an opening at which starts the Montcaire road.

We advance between olive groves and cultivated land, although on our right there already appears mountain vegetation in the form of a pine forest that covers the hillside of the Comuna de Fornalutx, also known as Puig de sa Bassa. Very soon and with no difficulties, we arrive close to the houses of the estate of **Bàlitx d'Amunt** (on top) that are about one hundred metres to our left.

An opening awaits us on the road that coincides with the change in the versant and it opens up a view of the magnificent valley of Bàlitx. We can see the houses of **Bàlitx d'Enmig** (in the middle) and, further away, the area of **Bàlitx d'Avall** (below) but not yet the houses. The valley is surrounded by steep mountains. The nearest mountainsides appear carpeted by the terraces of olive trees. We begin the descent, but soon we leave the road and take, on the right, the old paved road and whilst going along we can enjoy this magnificent example of traditional road paving. Next, in an ideal spot,

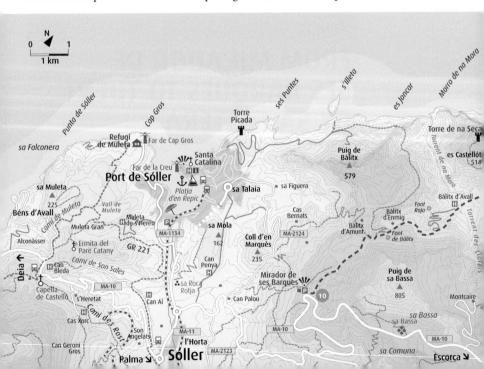

we come across the **spring of Bàlitx**, that has a genuine dry stone shaft and a false vault, typical of mountain springs, with an interior gutter that drains into a tank. Various elm trees and poplars complete the scene.

We continue going down, and five minutes from the spring are the recently restored houses of the estate of Bàlitx d'Enmig.

We continue along the cart track and, for the first time, even though distant, we see the houses of Bàlitx d'Avall, with the Torre de na Seca, the Coll de Biniamar and the mountain of Montcaire as a backdrop. At the fork that follows, one needs to pay a little attention: in front, with a tendency to the right, there is a new track for cars; on the left there is the cart track of the possessió, along which, after a few metres of having taken it (on the right, in a northerly direction) there is the continuation of the paved road. We link up with the track for cars just before reaching the houses that are well sited in the same centre of the large hollow, with the old circular fortified tower set in the architectural ensemble; it is the most notable part, together with the chapel that stands as an independent building.

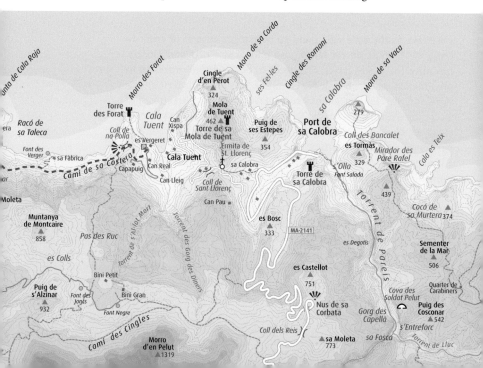

Bàlitx d'Enmig and Coll de Biniamar

We take to the walk again and go back a few metres in order to cross the **Torrent de na Mora**, also known as Bàlitx and Llorers. Just after the ascent starts, one needs to be careful in order not to miss the old road, called de Na Cavallera. It is paved in certain sections and runs to the right of a recent track. After a short stretch of steep slope, the old road is cut short, swallowed up by the new track along which we follow the ascent and very soon reach the highest part of the **Coll de Biniamar**.

We begin the short descent still by the same track that terminates immediately. We now find what is left of the paved road and a narrow path on the left that leads to the houses of **Sa Costera**. After a short time, the new landscape of the sea at our feet, with the houses on the left to the west, takes us by surprise. Further up, at the summit, the isolated **Torre de na Seca** kept a watch over the place and communicated with other neighbouring watchtowers. We continue to unravel the route of the Camí de sa Costera, a typical example of a bridle path that, always along the coast and sometimes very steep, runs between the sea at the very bottom and the rugged buttresses of the Montcaire mountain. The vegetation that accompanies us includes couch grass, gorse, grey leaved cistus and a few pine trees that survived the fires.

Further on we reach a badly signposted intersection; the road to the left goes to the **Font des Verger** or de la Costera. It is a path that has been invaded by vegetation and it descends very rapidly. The entrance to the complex, made up of the spring and the old electricity "factory", is via a small bridge; this passes over the canal with reeds that takes water from the spring to the large tank that used to control the flow of water to the turbine. Work has recently been undertaken to channel the water from the spring to Port de Sóller.

Returning on the Camí de sa Costera, after the steep ascent from the spring, we will stay on it until Tuent. It maintains a constant height, with a majestic route right on the mountainside. Once we are close to Morro del Forat, a short ascent will take us to the Coll de na Polla. A small pine wood makes way for an olive grove zone and just ahead we reach the houses of the estate of **Capapuig** (or Frapuig) that have recently been restored.

We just need to go down a short slope along a paved road to reach the first buildings of **Tuent**, on the Vergeret side. With the view of the beautiful cove, we end our excursion.

A waterfall in Sa Costera

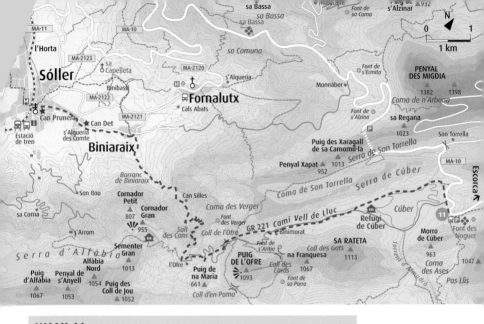

GULLY OF BINIARAIX

FROM CÚBER TO SÓLLER

Itinerary: Cúber opening (Ma-10, 34 km point) - Houses of Binimorat - Coll de l'Ofre - Houses of L'Ofre - Gully of Biniaraix - Biniaraix - Alqueria des Comte - Sóller

Rating: **Moderate**	Approximate time (without stops): **3 h 20 m**

We begin at the 34 km point milestone of the Pollença-Andratx road. At this point we find the opening of the tarmac road that skirts around the **reservoir of Cúber**. Our route can continue along the wide and asphalted path of the dam and reservoir, which coincides with the path of the houses of Ofre and Lluc to Sóller. It is best, however, to take the new route of the **GR-221**, which advances on the right (west) of the reservoir. Thus, on the left we have the water course; we pass a gully formed of cement and the path rises over two sides. On the left, on the other side of the water, stands the Morro de Cúber, which has a deforested appearance. On the right we can see a lime kiln, and some ten minutes later we reach the end of the reservoir with the Cúber refuge, a small modern construction.

After the refuge, we see the wide path on our left: before reaching it we come across a metal gate in the crossing wall that marks the entrance to the **Binimorat** and **Ofre** properties; in front of our path is a pedestrian pass while the wide gate is further away to the right. After the gateway, our path links up with the wide path

Very soon we pass another metal gate with a small pine wood and small abandoned terraces on the left. Brambles, thistles, sarsaparilla, spurge, and asphodel, amongst other species, make up the vegetation on the sides of the road. After an opening without a gate, in a transverse wall, we reach the house of Binimorat. This is a sober and isolated mountain building. It retains its lovely Arabic farm place name, that was documented in 1231.

Near Binimorat, before a stream, we follow the road on the right. The **Font de l'Aritja** is further away from us, to the left of the wide path. We continue the climb to **Coll de l'Ofre** by the road, between pine trees and the occasional holm oak. A quarter of an hour after leaving Binimorat, we reach the Coll de l'Ofre, the highest part of the route.

Coll de l'Ofre

On the right there is an iron cross, whilst on the left there rises the conical silhouette of the peak.

From the Coll we drop down towards the houses of Ofre. Near to the Coll, a path leaves on the left that goes to Coll d'en Poma, the **Font del Broll** and with one of the peak paths. The descent to the Pla (plain) de l'Ofre shows, like the climb, two different paths: the old path, metalled, which cuts the long bends of the second, more modern path, and suitable for vehicles. The old path and road intertwine in the high part, but immediately the old path is to the left of the pass. Further down, the old path merges with the modern track, towards the right. A detour for pedestrians takes us away from the new houses of Ofre, which we can see on our left, next to the Font de la Teula. They are small houses, adapted to the setting, with cages for different species of birds. Further on, discretely off our path, are the old **houses of Ofre**, more rustic and severe, and still abandoned today.

Towards the northeast, the perspective widens in the direction of the Biniaraix ravine and Sóller. Our path drops until joining the real path of the Biniaraix ravine, which we take to the right. The first section is a road, with a wall on the right. One hundred metres further on, after a metal gate, the Biniaraix ravine begins in earnest. The path adopts the typical aspect of a mountain path, stony and staggered. At the start, the road runs alongside the torrent that flows on the left. However, it soon reaches the first steep slope and the torrent falls headlong at the point known as **Salt dels Cans** (dog's jump). The road encircles the precipice on the right and offers us a good visual description of the slope. After passing the jump, we cross another metal gate, from which the road remains paved and constantly staggered.

As we gradually descend, olive trees appear together with the elaborate and bold terraces that support them. On the right slope, one should observe the wide stony ground of Verger. At about half an hour from the Salt dels Cans gate, we leave on the left the Gorg d'en Catí road, a beautiful spot, especially when the torrent carries water. Further down, at about five or six minutes from the previous crossing, we arrive next to the only houses, apart from the huts, that appear all along the road between the Ofre houses and the small village of Biniaraix.

The handful of small buildings that make up the hamlet of the **Biniaraix gully** —the property is currently divided up— are situ-

Camí de Biniaraix

ated near the fork that leads to the Font des Verger or in the same road of the spring. When they are left behind, the Verger torrent appears. The road crosses it via a paved ford; there are also stepping stones and a small rustic wooden bridge. Later, still at a short distance from the houses, the **Verger torrent** meets that of Barranc. Continuing ahead, we reach a second ford, with a stone on the right and a small bridge with a stepping stone on the right and a small cement bridge on the left. From here one sees **S'Estret**, a beautiful shady spot sitting in a gorge. A small bridge situated at the entrance leaves the torrent on the left; however, both road and torrent will continue to interweave.

After passing the Estret, the torrent becomes deeper and forms a river basin. In the meantime, the road continues and the twists and turns become more noticeable. We go past a hut in ruins and cross the torrent via a new ford with a stepping stone on the right and a cement bridge on the left. Further on, among olive trees, we leave the road of the cave of S'Alova, (a talayotic burial site) and the cave of Ses Alfàbies on the left.

A little further on we reach the spring, modernized with concrete, and at the next bend, we can already contemplate the nearby small village of **Biniaraix**, with the houses of the estate of Can Ribera and the large tower that identify it in the foreground. We cross the last ford, which has a concrete bridge on the right and a stepping stone on the left. The paving of the road disappears just before entering the village. We enter Biniaraix by the typical washhouse and the houses of the estate of **Cas Don**, that have a façade adorned with a large baroque shield of the Bauçà family coat of arms. On the right we have the parish church of the Puríssima. At the last house of Biniaraix, called **Es Pujador**, a small flight of steps takes us once again onto the tarmac, in order for us to continue towards Sóller, between houses, farmyards and orange groves.

Prior to entering Sóller, we pass by the outskirts of the **Alqueria des Comte**, always next to the torrent that is now markedly wide. On the right, the road that comes from Fornalutx links up with that of Biniaraix. A few more metres' walk and we have already entered the town centre via Carrer de l'Alqueria des Comte and that of La Lluna. In this way, we pass in front of interesting buildings such as **Can Prunera**, which is modernist in style (now **Museu del Modernisme**), and the **Casa de la Lluna**. We then enter Sóller's square to end the itinerary.

The Puig Roig and Morro de Sa Vaca in the background

WALK 12

LA VOLTA AL PUIG ROIG
(THE WALK ROUND THE PUIG ROIG)

Itinerary: Lluc-Pollença road (Ma-10, Pollença-Andratx) km 15.8 - Houses of Mossa - Coll dels Ases - Pas d'en Segarra - Font del Nespler - Es Cosconar - Porxo del Pinar - Son Llobera - Can Pontico - Clot d'Albarca - Lluc

| Rating: **Difficult** | Approximate time (without stops): **4 h 25 m** |

Notice: since this excursion goes through private land, access will only be permitted on Sundays.

We set off at the 15.3 km point of the Ma-10 road, that is about 3 kilometres from Lluc in the direction of Pollença. At this point we come to the gate and the beginning of the **Camí de Mossa**, to the left of the road if we are going towards Pollença. The route begins dropping slightly towards the valley of Mossa, with lots of olive groves. The view of **Puig Caragoler de Femenia** dominates the panorama. We leave a path to the left that approaches Lluc and continues going slightly to the right.

The road remains flat and leaves, on the right, one of the roads that goes to Mosset. Then it crosses a small stream with stone defences and forks to the right. Very soon we can make out the houses that stand out on a hillock.

After a little more than ten minutes of the route, we reach an opening with a wooden gate and another smaller one on the right for pedestrians A few metres further along, where there is a loose rock that occupies the corner of the fork, we see on our left another road that goes along the **Sementers de Mossa**. On the right we leave away that leads to Mosset and which forms an acute angle with our route. Before reaching the **houses of Mossa**, we take a detour on a recently built path, which avoids passing in front of the houses; the new way is signposted with a poster that indicates "Puig Roig" and crosses the climb to a slope with steps. The path goes round and behind the houses and climbs through the holm-oak wood.

When we have recovered our way, we see that we are dealing with a good bridle path that passes along oak trees and a retaining wall on the left. Along this road, a little more than five minutes after

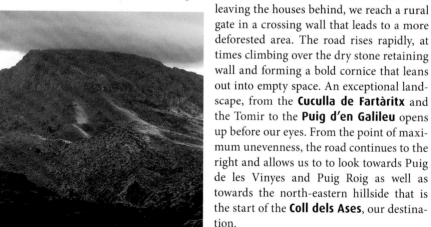

Puig Roig

leaving the houses behind, we reach a rural gate in a crossing wall that leads to a more deforested area. The road rises rapidly, at times climbing over the dry stone retaining wall and forming a bold cornice that leans out into empty space. An exceptional landscape, from the **Cuculla de Fartàritx** and the Tomir to the **Puig d'en Galileu** opens up before our eyes. From the point of maximum unevenness, the road continues to the right and allows us to to look towards Puig de les Vinyes and Puig Roig as well as towards the north-eastern hillside that is the start of the **Coll dels Ases**, our destination.

Reaching the pass, we discover a new panorama, that of the northern slope of the mountain with direct views over the seas. The Coll appears very deforested; towards the northeast there is the Puig Caragoler de Femenia.

From here we continue our walk, now along the hillside of Puig Roig. The road is similar to the one we have followed from Mossa. Approximately ten minutes later we come across a water trough known by the name of **Cocó de la Balma**. It is shaped like a small square pond, with the rock part completely irregular. The road, stuck to the hillside, tries to move away from the precipices and the hollows that nose-dive towards the sea. The vegetation is poor though there are examples of olive-blossom, thistle, asphodel, sarsaparilla and Balearic Saint John's wort as well as other species. Further on we leave, on the left, an open cave in the vertical rock, next to which the road has a double retaining wall. Broom and some ivy are added to the vegetation species. Thus, after a few twists and turns, the last with a rock on the right and a hollow, we reach the **Pas d'en Segarra**.

The pass is an important part of the itinerary, as it represents the maximum point of inflection to the north of the Volta; the natural wall of rock falls vertically over the road and it has to adopt the form of a rocky cornice in order to negotiate the difficult obstacle. We also come across remains of old corrals in the landscape.

From the Pas d'en Segarra, we continue with the itinerary and, on a light descent, its direction points west initially and then later southwest. The road, that leans out to sea, sticks to the cut out rock in order to avoid the unevenness. It adopts the form of a path and at the end it separates itself from the mountain massif; at approximately a quarter of an hour away from the Pas d'en Segarra, there appears at our feet **Cala Codolar** and the **Morro d'en Bordils**, a promontory that rises vertically from the level of the sea. On top of this crag one finds the Torre de Lluc, an old watchtower and defence tower dating from the beginning of the 17th century.

Whilst we continue towards the Des Nespler spring, the hollow is the central field of vision together with the Morro d'en Bordils. After a ring of wild olive trees, we reach a small pass of little more than one metre wide. It is uphill and not difficult, though one is obliged to use one's hands to climb up it; immediately afterwards one needs to be careful as a landslip of the terrace leads one to think that the path goes downhill, when in reality it is better to negotiate it on the left and get back to the path on the other side. In the meantime, there appears in front of our eyes the **Puig Major** massif. Between couch grass, lentisk and Saint John's wort, we reach a depression formed by the watercourses that plunge down from the **Roca Roja** (846m); we cross two small streams and reach the opening of the **Nespler spring**; the opening is in a wall where we can still see the remains of a wooden jump. The opening indicates the presence of the spring that is hidden and can be found about forty metres further up, on our left.

We follow the road that starts to drift southwards. Very soon we can see the construction called the police barracks, recently restored. We leave on the right a few paths that lead to the barracks and also link up with the **Des Poll spring**. We pass between hillsides of couch grass that descend from the Roca Roja, and a few small streams that flow down the slope below. Thus we reach an opening in the transverse wall, behind which we can see the Des Poll spring, situated at a lower position to ours. The road, that skirts around the high wall of this slope, will take us to the houses of the estate of Cosconar. A few minutes later the slope evens out and allows us to see a group of wild olive trees on the right. The panoramic view now allows us to discover the formidable gully of the **Torrent de Pareis**. Behind, dominating the panorama, is the **Puig Major de Son Torrella** and, on the left, the pointed **Puig de les Vinyes** (1,103m).

We soon catch sight of the houses of the estate of **Cosconar**, after a change of direction towards the east. To reach them we have to take, on the right, a wider road that comes from the barracks and the spring. It is an authentic troglodyte dwelling, built in a large natural cave and closed only by a large parament that serves as a façade.

We continue towards Lluc on a cart track that has a few olive trees next to it. We pass a small esplanade and two bends and we abandon, on the left, the path that goes to S'Hort de la Plana and then links up again to the houses of the estate of Mossa; another turn, this time to the left, takes us to a spot with a wide panoramic view, with the steep hillside of Puig Roig on the left and the basin of the Torrent de Lluc on the right. In the meantime, Puig Tomir appears in front of us and nearer, a part of the **Albarca valley**. We descend

Clot d'Albarca

slowly, firstly along a stretch with a north-easterly tendency until we pass around the riverbed of a watercourse after a large solitary pine tree. A little after the watercourse, we pass an opening without a gate in a transverse wall, with a ring of pine trees behind that are followed by wild olive trees. The descent soon speeds up in the form of a series of bends; the first is on the left and is quite open and takes us to another opening without a gate, after which the tight twists and turns start. Some can be negotiated by short cuts that have marked paths that go through plantations of almond, fig and olive trees. The last stretch of short cuts that leaves the cart track on the right with a turn to the left, ends with a steep descent with three steps; after that we can see the **Porxo des Pinar**.

We follow the road, with olive trees planted on small terraces and surrounded by fine and stony earth. Soon we pass an opening and, further ahead, we leave a spring on the left. Next we pass another opening without a gate. From here the road descends slightly, with a few gentle bends and with the houses of the estate of Ses Tosses that can be seen rising on the right. At about seven or eight minutes from the previous opening, we come across another one without a gate. Just after, on the left, there appears another olive storage shed. Very near there is an opening that has an iron chain to prevent vehicles from crossing but not walkers. At about thirty metres there is another opening, but this time with a wooden gate. A little further we leave, on the left, the entrance of the Sa Plana estate. We then pass a small stream framed by stone and eucalyptus trees, whilst on the right, surrounding the Torrent de Lluc, there is a dense oak wood. In this way we reach the height of Ca s'Escrivà, a house that rises on our left. Then, very near, we come across the **Alqueda torrent** that just after merges its waters with those of the Lluc torrent. The road crosses it further on, but we can cross the banks directly via a small concrete bridge with iron sides that appears on our right. A few metres further on we go beyond the opening that has a metal gate from which follows the rear wall of a building. Now, on a tarmac road, we enter one of the most inhabited vicinities of the Clot d'Albarca. First of all, we leave the Cas Secretari house on the left, then we pass a wooden gate and enter the **Can Pontico** area.

A little further along, on the right, there appears the entrance of **Son Llobera**, with a covered well. We then pass an opening with a metal gate and cross a watercourse, via a bridge, that is just a few metres away from the confluence of this watercourse with the Torrent de Llluc. Now the road runs flat through the centre of the **Clot d'Albarca**; further on, on our left, the zone called **S'Aram** stretches out. Here copper mining took place. A group of poplars indicates the Clot de ses Cireres, whilst further up, the uneven crags of the Pixarells close the valley. At about five minutes from the last opening, we pass another and reach, a few minutes later, the opening of the *possessió* of Albarca, with a wooden gate and a pass for walkers on the left. Nearby there is a small esplanade with olive trees and one can see different elements of an hydraulic system, such as a small wall with a channel and an irrigation ditch with dry stone channels. Just after, we pass a small bridge that crosses the **Torrent de Lluc**. On the left there is a row of poplar trees and on the right there are fruit trees, mainly fig trees, and behind them we can catch a glimpse of the houses of the estate of Albarca. After a few metres that tend to go to the left, the road turns slightly to the right and heads directly to the houses; on the right meanwhile, the Puig Roig stands out. At the next bend on the left we leave the houses' road on the right; from this point one has a better view of the architecture, that includes an old defence tower.

The roof of Majorca from Puig Roig

The road has various turns, after which we pass a small bridge over a watercourse. We can take a paved short cut with steps that goes towards the right. A little further up it links up again with the tarmac road and the start of the next bend continues up towards the right and heads towards an opening in a dry stone wall that we go through to enter the oak wood. Further up we retake the tarmac road towards the right. Two bends further up we take the last stretch of the short cut again on the left; it ends with eleven uneven steps that take us once again to the wide road, along which we go towards the left. About two minutes later we reach an opening and we advance up a slight ascent; this is the final stretch of the excursion. Next there is a bridge that crosses the Torrent de Lluc, whose course here is very deep, and we can see a small embankment, along which we move closer to **Lluc**, with the **Camí dels Misteris** (the road of mysteries) on the left, and an access road on the right, until we reach the pilgrim's square and the sanctuary.

Font de Muntanya

WALK 13

CAMÍ VELL FROM LLUC TO POLLENÇA

Itinerary: The Ma-10 road, 17.4 km point - The Cross of Menut - Houses of Menut - Houses of Binifaldó - Font de Muntanya - Les Voltes - Ca l'Hereuet - Houses of Son March - Pi de Son Grua (Ma-10, km 5.3)

| Rating: **Easy** | Approximate time (without stops): **2 h 45 m** |

We start the itinerary at the 17.4 km point of the Pollença to Lluc road (Ma-10). On the right, (if you come from Lluc), there is an opening on the Menut and Binifaldó tarmac road that coincides with the Camí Vell from Lluc to Pollença. Two minutes after starting the walk, we see the **Creu de Menut** on the right. The old gothic style religious symbol protects, from this point, walkers and the houses of the estate of **Menut** that one reaches about two minutes later on the right of the road. Currently, forest rangers occupy the houses where plantations of natural interest are cultivated. The houses form a complex collection of architectural buildings. The defence tower has a square ground plan.

We leave Menut via a metal gate, after which we take the tarmac road that goes slightly uphill. The tree vegetation is made up of a mixture of pine trees and oaks, accompanied by rockroses, lentisk and spurges. Rising on our left, Puig Roig and Puig Caragoler de Femenia dominate the landscape, whilst on the right, there are the hillsides of Moleta de Binifaldó. About eight minutes later and having passed a transverse wall with no opening, we reach the height of **Font des Còssil**, that is a few metres away on our right; on the left there is a reservoir that is fed by the spring. A little further on we reach the very tall poplar trees that announce the presence of the Torrent d'Alqueda and the houses of the estate of **Binifaldó**, situated on the right. A sign tells us that this path forms part of the **Ruta de Pedra en Sec** (Dry stone route), the **GR-221** (Grand Rondonée). Here we deviate a few metres away from our itinerary, along the tarmac road that goes up to the Font des Pedregaret bottling plant in order to visit it.

The houses of the estate of Binifaldó are situated at the foot of Puig Tomir and are surrounded by tall oak trees and farmland. They are public property and are currently used as a nature school. From the houses we return to the poplar trees of the torrent and get back to our position and original direction towards Pollença. The Camí Vell turns to the left, if we are coming from Menut, after crossing the torrent, and it is now flat and not asphalted, with the hillock of Puig Tomir on the right. On the left we have the **Alzina** (holm oak) **d'en Pere**, a singular tree for both its size and age. We pass a gate that places us in the area of Ses Rotes Velles, an old farming area tied to Binifaldó. We reach a second opening, wide and gateless, in a dry stone wall; we also see in the vicinity examples of rock roses. Next, we pass a watercourse and reach the **Font Negra** area. The spring is somewhat separated from the road, on the left, behind a dry stone wall, with reeds and an irregular shaped trough; a covered small canal connects it to a very rustic well. Next we reach an opening with concrete posts and a metal gate with a walker's crossing on the left; on the right there is a forest track. Further on, we pass a torrent and continue slightly downhill; there are a few bends and there is a recently built irrigation ditch. This way we reach the intersection of the road with the houses of the estate of **Muntanya** towards the left. A stop is opportune at this intersection in order to admire the view towards the bay of Pollença and the panorama over the houses of the estate of Muntanya, that we see practically at our feet, with the Puig Gros de Ternelles as a backdrop. From the intersection of the houses, we continue on the right along the Camí Vell, but we soon leave the wide path and, on the right, take the road rehabilitated as a footpath. This is a small lesson in public thoroughfare history between Pollença and Lluc; the cart track is the old 19th-century path, while the metalled road is the way of medieval origin. Both paths intertwine at several points. After dropping down we reach the **Font de Muntanya**. It has an interesting mine with a mouth in a semicircular arch; the return from the mine has a high section, with a side channel, and another section, lower, which goes into the spring. On the right of the spring there are stone benches and a rustic table, also of stone, and, in the environs there are oak trees, cypress trees and reeds.

After having seen the spring, we follow the **Camí Vell**, along which we cross a small bridge that spans a torrent that has reeds and

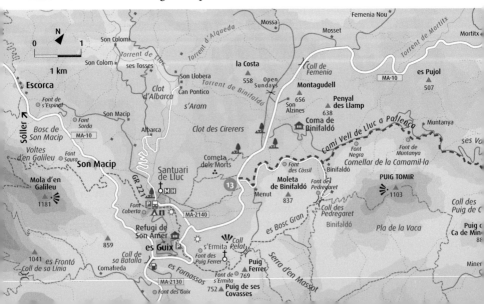

ferns. On the left we can see a sheep shed. Further on we reach a junction, which we take to the right, which shows 2 h 45 min to Pollença. The holm oak wood has several coal silos. With a small wall to the left, we reach the pass that separates the **Possessió de Muntanya**. We are in the district of Pollença and we now leave Escorca. The metalled road continues through the holm oak wood. Further down, to the left, is a carob tree and a lime kiln.

Some 25 minutes from the Muntanya pass, we reach the old cart track, which we take to the right. Looking left we see the continuation of the wide path, close to the **Ca l'Hereuet** pass, in an area that forms the entrance to the **Vall d'en March**. This path, which is not on our route, continues to a place called Les Voltes (the turns), since there are twenty-three bends on the climb up. We do not continue along the cart track, however, because we divert left, along the rehabilitated road. We go down and the terrain is rocky, on the left is a dry stone wall and on the right a metallic fence. A little further down, we link up with a wide path, with a sign identifying the **GR**. The holm oak wood gives way to agricultural land, immediately reaching the Can Melsion pass, with its natural stone posts and metal gate. The path then takes an almost ninety-degree turn to the right.

Next, we leave on the right, the Can Jordi opening and the Camí del Molinet. Also on the right is the Camí del Pujol, that links up

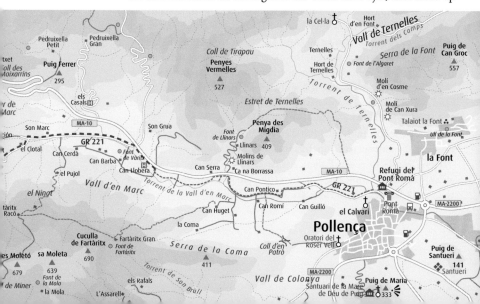

with that of Fartàritx. The houses of the estate of Pujol stand out and above one can also see the **Pla de Fartàritx** and the Coa del Cavall. We advance, without difficulty, along the centre of the Vall d'en March and, on the right, see a well that supplies water to the nearby fields. Close by we can see a group of poplar trees and it does not take us long to reach the houses of the estate of Son March, on the left of the road.

The present day *possessió* of **Son March** formed part of the farm called Binitiger in the Muslim era. In 1606 the property belonged to Llorenç March and the family name went on to be given to the valley and the *possessió*.

We continue still along the centre of the valley, on flat ground, with the Cuculla de Fartàrix and the Puig de Ca de Miner on the mountainous outline that follows on our right. At about five minutes away from the houses we reach the **Camp d'Avall** opening. The house has a sundial on its façade. The torrent de la Vall d'en March flows on the left and is separated from the road by a row of oak trees that gives the place a shady aspect. Next we pass in front of the Cal Xorc house and the Les Creus opening on the left.

Already on the final stretch of the excursion, we cross the torrent over a bridge that is located next to the houses of the estate of L'Hort de Son Grua and next, we leave a new bridge on the right that gives access to private villas. On the right of the wide and now asphalted road flows the torrent, whilst on the left we can see the lemon tree fields. We reach the **Son Grua pine tree** that is next to the Lluc to Pollença (Ma-10) main road at the 5.3 km point, where we consider the excursion ended. If we do not have a car waiting for us, we should continue following the signs of the **GR-221**. Close to the road, we reach the 2.8 km mark, where we return right, along the Cal Diable path. The path continues towards Pollença. We go alongside the torrent by the Pas d'en Barqueta bridge and reach the town, at the entrance of which is the Pont Romà refuge.

If one wants to reach Pollença, that is just over five kilometers away, one has to walk the first two kilometres along the road and then walk the rest again through the Camí Vell.

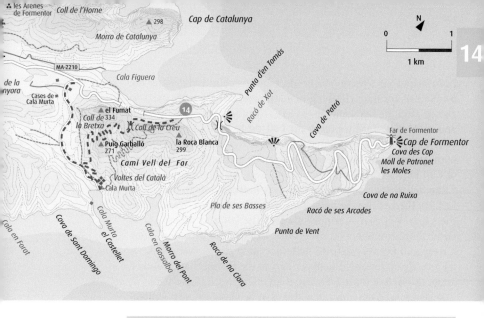

WALK 14

EL FUMAT

CAMÍ VELL OF FORMENTOR

Itinerary: Far de Formentor road, 14.3 km point - Camí vell del Far - El Fumat - Coll de la Bretxa - Cala Murta - Houses of Cala Murta

Rating: **Moderate**	Approximate time (without stops): **2 h 15 m**

We start the excursion on the Far de Formentor road (Ma-2210), after the Fumat tunnel exit and the 14 km milestone. We walk along tarmac for some three hundred metres, before reaching the Punta d'en Tomàs plain and just after a game reserve (one has to pay careful attention), we leave the road and turn right, going up the hillside in order to take the old road to the **Far de Formentor** that forms an acute angle to the road. We follow the traditional path from the link-up point, with a tendency to the right, towards the southwest; the way is a bridle path, with a retaining bank on the side of the slope, making its stones more evident as we advance.

The path climbs gently, between couch grass and gradually separates from the road that stays on the right; the north slope of the

Roca Blanca rises above our heads, with irregular walls. After ten minutes of constant climbing in a straight line, the path starts to zigzag; after the first bend on the left, five others follow, to the right and to the left, until we reach the **Coll de la Creu** (238m), named after the cross that was carved in a rock to signal the halfway point of the path's route. Here new views open up, namely in the direction of Cap Pinar, in the background, and over the continuation of the Camí Vell, that goes up to the Coll de la Bretxa. Close to the pass of La Creu there is also the point known as Salt del Moro. We abandon the Camí Vell that continues towards the left and we set out to climb to the summit of Fumat (334m). In a westerly direction, along a steep and not very defined path that often passes over rocks, we go directly up towards the upper part of the **Fumat** that is reached about thirteen or fourteen minutes after leaving the Camí Vell.

Once reaching the summit, with a clear geodesic top, one contemplates a large panoramic view. The vegetation that surrounds the summit is basically made up of couch grass, rosemary, broom, fan palms, asphodels, lentisk, sarsaparilla and Balearic Saint John's wort. Apparently the name *Fumat* (smoked) comes from the blackish spots, that seem like smoke marks, that appear on the cut walls of the peak.

Puig del Fumat

We descend from the Fumat summit along the same road used to climb up it; there is no concrete route at the start and there is a very undefined path further down. Reaching again the Coll de la Creu, we get back on the Camí Vell, now with a tendency to the right from the descent position; this stretch descends in a continuous zigzag. Six bends further down, one passes beneath the overhead electricity cables that feed the lighthouse, and a few minutes later there are no more bends; we link up with the riverbed that shelters the Torrent de les Agulles. The torrent flows down rapidly towards the left in the direction of Cala en Gossalba. At this point of inflection, the road starts to rise with a marked zigzag towards the **Coll de la Bretxa** (245m). The bends that face south offer us new perspectives over Cala en Gossalba. Leaving behind these twists and turns, we finally link up with this second pass and see that it forms a small gorge or an open pass in the rock, in the shape of a breach made by a drilling bit, hence its name.

We go down the western hillside of the Fumat and the **Puig Garballó**. During this descent, the road takes a spectacular route, with continuous and emphatic twists and turns; we count up to 30 prior to linking up with the Cala Murta beach. In the first stretch these bends are tighter, however as we gradually descend they become more open each time adapting themselves to the inclination of the slope. Despite its beauty, the landslips and the vegetation invasions, nearly always the result of fires, are taking over this road and its winding route.

Whilst we are unravelling twists and turns, we are surrounded by brushwood vegetation, without the presence of tree specimens. At about twenty minutes from the pass, we reach a rounded spur in the shape of a ridge that separates two small inclines that are, in fact, folds of the Puig Garballó; on the left, towards the south, the road continues to Cala Murta; further to the right, towards the northwest, one can descend in a more direct way to the houses of the estate of Cala Murta and this is a way of cutting short the excursion. We decided on our itinerary the descent to the cove, thus we retake the Camí Vell del Far towards the left, where more bends await us; these bends here are known as **Les voltes del Català** (the Catalan bends). One should not be surprised that the Camí Vell continues towards the cove, as at this cove there was a small jetty at the time of building the lighthouse, for loading and unloading materials and people and also it was used later for the maintenance of the lighthouse.

On this new course, there soon appear the first pine trees, situated preferentially on the closest hillside of the river bed, that which is furthest away from the cove. After two bends we already see **Cala Murta**, an image of great landscape interest. Further down, at about fifteen minutes from the fork, the road crosses a stream and is equipped with a retaining bank, erected with bigger stones, that passes over the stream. We are very close to the cove, on the final stretch of the Camí Vell, that appears very damaged by the land-slips. At about four minutes from the watercourse, amongst agaves, we pass a wire fence that marks the enclosure of the villa; meanwhile the cove stretches below our feet. On building the villa the road was interrupted, thus the third from last bend skirts round the building. The next turns to the left and, close to the coastline, the last one takes us to the cove's beach. If the way Is closed, we will have to go down to the right, to link up with the main path of the cove. It is a recent and irregular diversion that crosses the slope parallel to the railing of the chalet, which is on our left. On reaching the wide path, we go to the left and immediately reach Cala Murta.

The waters of Cala Murta open up to the southeast; there is a pebble beach and a natural image that is only broken by the villa on the north-eastern slope. On the ground side, a row of pine trees with rushes and lentisk, aligns itself in front of the coast; on the left side, if we have our backs to the sea, there are a few benches and tables for visitor's use.

We abandon the cove and set out to go up the road of the houses. After a first bend on the right, we pass the Torrent de Cala Murta and link up with the tarmac of the road that starts next to a small building close to the beach. Very soon we leave, on the left, ruins of buildings, and we cross a poorly signed opening that is followed by pine trees, palm hearts, myrtle and rosemary. A little further up we cross the torrent three more times via the corresponding small bridges that cross its course. In this stretch there are young oak trees and myrtles, the *murtes* that give the cove its name. At approximately eight or nine minutes from the beach, one needs to leave a cart track on the left that goes up to the second camping area of Cala Murta, that does not have fixed facilities. We continue going up along the main asphalted road. Very near, on the right, we pass the youth campsite, at which point the road bends to the right; after an opening we reach the **houses of the estate of Cala Murta**, next to the road, on its 13 km point which is the final point of the excursion.

PRACTICAL GUIDE

Popular festivals, museums, wine cellars and restaurants, accommodation, markets and fairs, arts and crafts, transport... In the practical guide we will find all the information needed to plan our stay in the Serra de Tramuntana.

Foguerons and demons, Festival of Sant Antoni

MUSEUMS AND CULTURAL CENTERS

BUNYOLA
Gardens of Alfàbia
Palma-Sóller road, km 17
Tel. +34 971 61 31 23
Open Monday to Friday from 9.30
a.m. to 6.30 p.m.; Saturdays until
1 p.m. (see page 97).

Gardens of Raixa
Palma-Sóller road, km 12,5
Tel. +34 971 21 97 41
visitesraixa@conselldemallorca.net
Re-opened after a recent reform.
Open on Saturdays and Sundays
from 10 a.m. to 2 p.m. (see p. 94).

DEIÀ
Col·lecció Son Marroig
Valldemossa-Deià road
Tel. +34 971 63 91 58
Open 9.30 a.m. to 2 p.m. and
3 p.m. to 5.30 p.m. In winter.
9.30 a.m. to 8 p.m. in summer.
Closed Sundays (see page 103).

Casa-Museu Robert Graves
Tel. +34 971 63 61 85
From April to October open Monday
to Friday from 10 a.m. to 5 p.m and
Saturdays until 3 p.m. November,
February and March, Monday to
Friday from 9 a.m. to 2 p.m. and
Saturdays until 2 p.m. The Robert
Graves Museum is in the **Ca n'Alluny**
estate, built in 1932 by Robert
Graves, where visitors can discover
the life and work of the writer.
www.fundaciorobertgraves.org

ESCORCA
Museu de Lluc
Sanctuary of Lluc
Tel. +34 971 87 15 25
Open every day; from 10 a.m. to
2 p.m. Daily performances of the
Blauets choir at 11.15 a.m. and
4.45 p.m. (see page 107).

ESPORLES
La Granja
Esporles-Puigpunyent road, km 2
Tel. +34 971 61 00 32
www.lagranja.net

Wednesdays and Fridays, handicraft and folklore show. Open
every day; from 10 a.m. to 6 p.m.
in winter and until 7 p.m. in summer (see page 99).

FORNALUTX
Can Xoroi
Oil press and painted tiles.
Carrer de sa Font, 8
Tel. +34 971 63 19 01
Open Friday and Saturday from
10.30 a.m. to 1.30 p.m.

POLLENÇA
Museu Municipal
Convent of Sant Domingo
Tel. +34 971 53 11 66
17th-century pottery, 19th-century
paintings and archaeological exhibits. In winter, open from Tuesday to
Sunday, from 11 a.m. to 1 p.m.; in
summer, also on Mondays, and the
afternoons, from 5 to 8 p.m.

SÓLLER
**Museu Balear de Ciències
Naturals-Jardí Botànic**
Palma-Sóller road, km 30
Tel. +34 971 63 40 64. Open from
10 a.m. to 6 p.m. Sundays: 10 a.m.
to 2 p.m. Closed on Mondays.

Museu de Sóller
Carrer del Mar, 13
Tel. +34 971 63 14 65
Ethnology, archaeology and an
interesting collection of masks.
Check opening times.

Museu Modernista Can Prunera
Carrer de sa Lluna, 90
Tel. +34 971 63 89 73
Cultural centre. Permanent collection of contemporary art (see
page 40). Check times.
www.canprunera.com

VALLDEMOSSA
Centre Cultural Costa Nord
Av. de Palma, 6
Tel. +34 971 61 24 25
Open every day
www.costanord.com

Fundació Cultural Coll Bardolet
Carrer Blanquerna, 4
Tel. +34 971 61 29 83
Permanent exhibition of the paint-
ing collection by the artist Josep
Coll Bardolet.

Museu Monestir de Miramar
Valldemossa-Deià road, km 2
Tel. +34 971 61 60 73
Open 9 a.m. to 5 p.m. except
Sundays (see page 101).

**Reial Cartoixa de Valldemossa
and Palau del Rei Sanç**
Plaça de la Cartoixa, 1
Tel. +34 971 61 21 06
April to September; 9.30 a.m.
to 6.30 p.m. October and March;
9.30 a.m. to 5.30 p.m. November
and February; 9.30 a.m. to 5 p.m.
December and January; 9.30 a.m.
to 3 p.m. Sundays 10 a.m. to
1.30 p.m. (see page 91).

F. Chopin and George Sand Cell
Cell 4, Cartoixa de Valldemossa
Tel. +34 696 40 59 92
December and January from
10 a.m. to 3.30 p.m. November,
February and March from 10 a.m.
to 4.30 p.m. April, May, June,
September and October from
10 a.m. to 6 p.m. July and August
from 10 a.m. to 6.30 p.m.
Sundays from 10 a.m. to 2 p.m.

Convent of Sant Domingo, Pollença

POPULAR FESTIVALS

CALENDAR

SANT ANTONI
January 17th
Mancor de la Vall: *foguerons* (bonfires), on the night before, and *Davallada des Corb* (a popular representation of an episode in the life of the saint); **Pollença**: *foguerons* and *Davallada del Pi*. Bonfires also in **Sóller**. Blessing of animals in all the towns.

SANT SEBASTIÀ
January 20th
Pollença: *Ball de les Taules*, a dance performed by the *Cavallets* ("small horses").

MARE DE DÉU DE LOURDES
February 11th
Sóller: *Processó de ses Torxes* (torch procession).

GOOD FRIDAY
Date subject to change
Pollença: *Processó del Davallament* (procession of the Descent), at the Calvari. This procession also takes place in **Valldemossa**.

EASTER MONDAY
Date subject to change
Pilgrimages to various chapels: Puig de Maria in **Pollença**, Cristo Rey in **Selva**, and **Binibona**.

TUESDAY AFTER EASTER
Date subject to change
Pilgrimage to the hermitage of Sant Miquel, in **Campanet**, with *Pujada des Pi* (the raising of a pine tree) and to the chapel of Santa Llúcia in **Mancor de la Vall**.

WEDNESDAY AFTER EASTER
Date subject to change
Pilgrimage to the hermitage of Cocó in **Lloseta**.

SUNDAY AFTER EASTER
Date subject to change
Pilgrimages to the castle of Sant Elm (**Andratx**), Puig de Son Seguí in Santa María del Camí, and to the chapel of La Trinitat (**Valldemossa**).

SANT JORDI'S
Saturday First Saturday after April 23rd
Festivities in honour of the patron saint in **Orient**.

PILGRIMAGE IN SA COMUNA
May 1st
At **Biniamar**, la Barrera d'Alt.

FESTES DE LA CREU
May 3rd
Local festivities in **Selva**.

PILGRIMAGE TO THE HERMITAGE OF MARISTEL·LA
First Sunday in May (and the last in August)
In **Esporles**.

SA FIRA DE SÓLLER
Second Sunday in May
In **Sóller**.

ES FIRÓ
Monday after the Fira Monday following the second Sunday in May
In **Sóller** and **Port de Sóller**, with *Moors and Christians*.

PROCESSÓ DE SES ÀGUILES
First Sunday after Corpus Christi. Date subject to change, May or June
In **Pollença**.

SANT JOAN
June 24th
Festivities in **Deià** and **Mancor de la Vall**.

SANT PERE
June 29th
Festivities in honour of the patron saint in **Andratx** and procession of boats in **Port d'Andratx**. Street party in the **Dels Amunt** neighbourhood in **Alaró**. Festivities also in **Escorca**, **Esporles**, **Port de Pollença** and **Port de Sóller**.

MARE DE DÉU DE LA MAR (OUR LADY OF THE SEA)
1st Sunday in July
In **Cala Sant Vicenç**.

SANTA VICTÒRIA
First weekend in July
In **Campanet**, with a slingshot competition.

CHORAL CONCERT AT THE TORRENT DE PAREIS
Second Sunday in July
At **sa Calobra**, by the Capella Mallorquina.

OUR LADY OF CARME
July 16th
Maritime processions in **Port d'Andratx** and **Port de Pollença**; festivities in honour of the patron saint also in **Es Capdellà**.

SANTA MARGALIDA
July 20th
Local festivities in **Santa Maria del Camí**.

SANT JAUME
July 25th
Open air dance in **Port des Canonge** and local festivities in **Calvià**.

SANTA ANNA
July 26th
Festa del Fadrí (Bachelor's fiesta), in **Moscari**.

PROCESSION *DEL CARRO TRIOMFAL DE LA BEATA*
July 28th
In **Valldemossa**.

SA PATRONA
August 2nd
In **Pollença**. *Els Cossiers*, ancient medieval dance, and *Moors and Christians*, in commemoration of the victory of Pollença over the corsair Dragut.

VERGE DE LES NEUS
August 5th
A popular fiesta in **Bunyola**.

SANT LLORENÇ
August 10th
Festivities in **Cala Tuent** and **Sa Calobra**, in honour of the patron saint in **Selva**, and for the Crowning of the Virgin Mary in **Lluc**.

PROCESSION DE LES CRESTES
August 14th
In **Valldemossa**.

ASSUMPTION OF OUR LADY
August 15th
Festivity in **Llucalcari, Puigpuny-ent, Caimari, Biniaraix, Port de Valldemossa** and the Vila Nova quarter in **Esporles**.

SANT ROC
August 16th
In **Alaró**
The end of the plague in 1653 is commemorated with a thanksgiving procession in the streets of Alaró and a dance by *Cossiers*.

SANT BARTOMEU
August 24th
Patron saint festivity. **Sóller** and **Valldemossa**.

FESTIVITY OF THE HOLY CHRIST
August 28th
In the hamlet of **S'Arracó**.

THE SLAUGHTER OF ST. JOHN THE BAPTIST
August 29th
Festivity in **Estellencs**.

FESTES DE MOSCARI
Last Sunday in August
Festivity in **Moscari**.

THE DISEMBARKATION OF JAUME I
September, 6th to 12th
In **Calvià**, *Moors and Christians*.

OUR LADY OF SEPTEMBER
September 8th.
Pilgrimage to the Castell d'**Alaró**; patron saint festivity in **Banyalbufar, Fornalutx** (*Festa des Bou*), **Lloseta, Galilea** and Mare de Déu de la Trapa festivity, in **S'Arracó**.

FESTIVITY OF SANTA MARIA
Second Sunday in September
In **Santa Maria del Camí**, with procession of carriages.

OUR LADY OF LLUC
September 12th
Festivity in the **sanctuary of Lluc**, with popular dances and the singing of vespers (*Vetlla de Santa Maria*) by the **Blauets** choir.

SANT MATEU
September 21th. In **Bunyola**.

SANTA TECLA
September 23th. In **Biniamar**.

SANT MIQUEL
September 29th. In **Campanet**.

SANTA CATALINA
November 25th
In **Bunyola**, with street bonfires.

CHRISTMAS
December 25th
Midnight Mass. (Misses del Gall). In all the towns of the Serra. One of the liveliest and most colourful is held in the **Sanctuary of Lluc**, with the *Anunci de l'Àngel* (annunciation of the angel) and the *Cant de la Sibil·la* (Song of the Sybil).

HANDICRAFTS

TYPICAL PRODUCTS

All the area has a great handicraft heritage. Many and varied hand-made objects can be found in the towns of the Serra de Tramuntana, amongst which stand out **vidre bufat** (blown glass) of various colours and designs; the hand-woven fabrics called **roba de llengos**; the delicate and complicated **brodats** (embroidery); the well known **siurells** (coloured terracotta whistles with amusing shapes); the **floreres** (dried flower compositions under crystal bells); **orange-wood cutlery; pottery, ceramics** and **basketwork**... The list of objects manufactured, as in the past, is very wide —there are also **picarols** (cowbells) and **espadrilles**—, and one can even speak at length about the miniscule masonry work in the **paret seca** (dry wall stone) that borders roads and contains terraces —this is consistently found all over the Serra. This has an artisan and heritage value and must be enjoyed in situ; it cannot be bought or taken home as a souvenir!

WHERE TO BUT HANDICRAFTS

ANTIQUES
SÓLLER
Toni de sa Coma
Vicari Pastor, 9 | Tel. +34 971 63 08 65

BRODATS (Embroidery)
POLLENÇA
Casa Maria
Pg. Saralegui, 86 (Port de Pollença)
Tel. +34 971 86 55 51

CERAMICS AND POTTERY
CAMPANET
Teulera de Can Dolç
Camí des Molins, 38
Tel. +34 971 51 63 88

LLOSETA
Sa Teulera. Pou Nou, 86
Tel. +34 971 51 47 66

LLUCMAJOR
Sa Teulera
Campos, 80 | Tel. +34 971 66 01 76

SANTA MARIA
Ca'n Bernat
Ramon Llull, 30
Tel. +34 971 62 13 06

SÓLLER
Castaldo Paris
Deià road, km 80
Tel. +34 971 63 09 31

Fet a Sóller - Estel Nou
Ses Marjades, 2
Tel. +34 971 63 39 42

POLLENÇA
Abco Colomar
Del Port road, Zone 4
Tel. +34 622 71 75 81

TRADITIONAL ICE CREAMS
SÓLLER
Sa Fàbrica de Gelats
Plaça des Mercat
Tel. +34 971 63 17 08

PICAROLS (Cowbells)
CAMPANET
Pascual Ros
Sa Carretera, 35
Tel. +34 971 51 60 76

ROBA DE LLENGOS
(Hand-woven fabrics)
LLOSETA
Art tèxtil Riera
Major, 50 | Tel. +34 971 51 40 34

POLLENÇA
Teixits Vicens
Roundabout Can Berenguer
Tel. +34 971 53 04 50

SANTA MARIA DEL CAMÍ
Art tèxtil Bujosa
Bernat Sta Eugènia, 53
Tel. +34 971 62 00 54

SIURELLS (Typical whistles)
CAMPANET
Pascual Ros
Sa Carretera, 35
Tel. +34 971 51 60 76

VIDRE (Blown glass)
CAMPANET
Menestralia
Alcúdia road, km 36
Tel. +34 971 87 71 04

S'ESGLEIETA (ESPORLES)
Lafiore
Valldemossa road, km 11
Tel. +34 971 61 18 00

Blown glass and *siurell*

MARKETS AND FAIRS

MARKETS

In all towns on market day, one can find the freshest fruit and vegetables of the area, clothes, tools for every job, as well as handicraft products described previously. In the area you can visit the following markets, but remember that in most cases they just set up stalls in the morning.

On Mondays there are markets in **Mancor de la Vall** and **Calvià**; on Tuesdays in **Alcúdia** and **Campanet**; on Wednesdays in **Andratx**, **Bunyola**, **Port de Pollença** and **Selva**; on Saturdays in **Alaró**, **Bunyola**, **Esporles**, **Lloseta** and **Sóller**; and on Sundays in **Alcúdia**, **Pollença** and **Valldemossa**. There is also a daily market in the Plaça dels Peregrins of the **Santuari de Lluc** that is open until five o'clock in the afternoon.

FAIRS

ANDRATX
First Sunday in April
In the castle of Son Mas (current town hall) and in the esplanade: livestock, agricultural machinery and handicrafts. There are also horse-riding displays and old carriages, as well as gastronomic displays and tasting.

CALVIÀ
Beginning of April
Goat and sheep fair, with shearing demonstrations, examples of farm tools and handicrafts. The main event is the morphological contest of Mallorcan breed sheep.

SANTA MARIA DEL CAMÍ
Last Sunday in April
Livestock, old vehicles, indigenous dog breeds, sampling... as well as alternative energy sources and ecological crops.

SÓLLER
La "Fira" and "el Firó"
Second Sunday in May and the immediate Monday after
If the Sunday fair is very interesting and diverse, the Monday el Firó awakes greater expectations, with the celebration of the mock battle between Moors and Christians.

CAMPANET
Second week in May
Exhibition of handicraft products where one can find baskets, rope-soled sandals, glassware items or *siurells*, amongst other things.

SELVA
"Fira de ses Herbes"
Second weekend of April
The first weekend after Saint John. The generic theme is the harvesting and traditional use of aromatic and medicinal plants.

ALCÚDIA
First Sunday in October
An exhibition of agricultural, stock-breeding and handicraft products of the island.

POLLENÇA
Second week in November
Agricultural and livestock show that is accompanied by a handicrafts exhibition in the convent cloister at which one can see embroidery, wicker chairs and stone cutting work on sandstone.

INCA
"Dijous bo"
Date variable
(Thursday in mid-November)
One of the most popular, appreciated and participated-in fairs of the island. Here one can come across almost anything and in quantity amongst the large number of participants and the multitude of stalls. In parallel, various festive activities are organized.

CAIMARI
"Fira de s'Oliva"
November
On the Sunday following the 18th, a fiesta is held that revolves around the olive and products deriving from it. An oil press is opened in order to show the process of obtaining oil and typical products are put on sale. At the same time, there are recitals of the olive workers own songs that are connected to the working of the fields in general.

SANTA MARIA DEL CAMÍ
"Festa del Vi novell"
November
Wine fair and open day at the cellars. Popular activities.

MANCOR DE LA VALL
"Fira de l'esclata-sang i de la Muntanya"
Last weekend of November
Dedicated to traditional mountain activities. Giants, devils, bestiary... Popular music and all kinds of traditional activities. Gastronomic seminars about the *esclata-sang* (*Lactarius sanguifluus*) wild mushroom).

GASTRONOMY AND RESTAURANTS

LET'S EAT!

Sitting down at a table to regain one's strength is the point where a traveller can most realise that he is in perfect symbiosis with the surroundings. Choosing the most appropriate food for each meal can also lead us to get to know this island better. Island food is simple, nutritious and genuinely Mediterranean: **pa amb oli** (slices of bread spread with tomatoes to blend with country cold cuts and olives), **arròs brut** (rice "dirtied" with hare and rabbit), **sopes mallorquines** (with seasonal vegetables and bread), **trempó** (pepper, onion, tomato and black olive salad with country olive oil), **tumbet** (a mixture of fried potatoes, peppers and aubergines covered with a tomato and onion sauce), **cocarrois** (with spinach, pine nuts and raisins)...

The gastronomy of the Serra de Tramuntana, based on fresh produce, fish, meat and seasonal vegetables, used to change according to the times of the year. Today, there is a year round supply of fruit and vegetables and so one can enjoy any dish at any time! Obviously though, the results on the palate will always be more satisfactory if food is consumed in accordance with natural production cycles.

Thus, although one can eat them all year round, the **sopes de matances**, are typical winter dishes. They are made with loin of pork, onions, garlic, tomatoes, cabbage, cauliflower, peas, mushrooms, artichokes and any other type of seasonal vegetables; to all this one adds the **sopes** (thin slices of brown bread). Everything is boiled together so that the stock is drunk and the dish is served dry. In summer *sopes* are much enjoyed.

These are made with garlic, onions, tomatoes, Swiss chard, young beans and green peppers; instead of boiling, they are blanched and served watery. Also very summery are **trempó** and **tumbet**, described previously, as well as **escalivada**, a cold mouthwatering mix of red peppers, aubergines and tomatoes that, after "sweating" in the oven, are peeled and cut into strips and served with a sprinkling of olive oil. And what can one say about aubergines and courgettes that are stuffed with either meat or seafood...?

Autumn dishes include **llampuga amb pebres** (common dolphinfish with peppers), **esclata-sangs torrats** (grilled milk-cap mushrooms) and products from pig slaughtering: **botifarrons, llonganissa, sobrassada**... When the **sobrassada** is served **amb suquet** (with sauce), it is served fresh, fried and sprinkled with honey.

Throughout the year one can eat **frit** (fried), that, as its name implies, is prepared by frying with different ingredients. We will cite three methods: the **frit de porc** (of pork) combines loin, bacon and pig liver, with potatoes, red peppers, garlic and milk-cap mushrooms all cut into small pieces; **frit de xot** or **de porcella**, with entrails (especially lungs) and the dried blood of a **xot** (a kid goat) or a **porcella** (a suckling pig), with garlic, potatoes, artichokes, peas, tender young broad beans, spring onions, fennel and any other vegetable at hand; and the **frit de marisc** (seafood), in which the previously mentioned meat is replaced by cuttlefish, squid, peeled prawns, monkfish, etc.

Other dishes worth tasting are **conill amb ceba** (rabbit cooked with onions), roast suckling pig, kid or suckling kid, loin of pork with cabbage and the popular **escaldums de pollastre** or **indiot** (chicken or turkey stews). As already mentioned, one of the most traditional dishes is **arròs brut**, a watery rice dish with meat and different types of vegetables and with a sauce that gives it its characteristic dark colour. Another very appreciated dish is snails, that are usually spicy and dipped into **allioli** sauce.

Regarding the cuisine of the sea produce, outstanding are stuffed squid, fish or spider crab rice and the exquisite results of preparing any fresh fish from our coast "a la mallorquina", that is, letting it cook in the oven, together with potatoes, onion, Swiss chard, spinach and spring onions. Majorcan lobster, highly appreciated, is only available during the summer months at fairly high prices.

There are dishes that, being typical of a certain town or that are prepared only at certain times or festive occasions, are out of reach of the visitor or only available to him at certain restaurants that try to make them known. However, in many Mallorcan homes, the preparation of many of those dishes continues: **greixonera d'Andratx, formatjada** (Pollença), **fava parada** and **coques de patata** (Valldemossa), **llet d'ametlla** (Santa Maria del Camí, for Christmas)... And as far as sweets and desserts are concerned, the range of sweets is notable. Apart from the famous **ensaïmada** there are cakes and pastries —**coques de torró, panellets, quartos, crespells, robiols, gató d'ametlla**...—, ice-creams —prickly pear, lemon, almond— bowls of curd cheese, fritters...

RESTAURANTS

If there are so many specialities the same thing can be said about restaurants and this makes it difficult to compile a complete and full list. The names and addresses of some of them are listed below, amongst which are the most outstanding and well known.

ALARÓ
Traffic
Pl. de la Vila, 6
Tel. +34 971 87 91 17
Sa Fonda
Can Ros, 4
Tel. +34 971 51 05 83

ANDRATX
Can Paco
Pere Seriol, 8
Tel. +34 971 17 79 08
Es Portal
Apotecari Gonzàlez, 12
Tel. +34 971 67 21 18
Mar Blau
Almirall Riera, 24
Port d'Andratx
Tel. +34 971 67 31 88

BANYALBUFAR
Son Tomàs
Baronia, 17
Tel. +34 971 61 81 49
Can Toni Moreno
Punta des Cavall, 2
Port d'es Canonge
Tel. +34 971 61 04 26

BUNYOLA
Sa Costa
Costa de s'Estació
Tel. +34 971 61 31 10
Es Garrigó
Bunyola - Santa Maria road, km 0.6
Tel. +34 971 61 50 39

CALVIÀ
Can Torrat
Major, 29-31
Tel. +34 971 67 06 82

CAMPANET
Can Gardo
Palma-Alcúdia road, km 36
Tel. +34 971 87 72 11
Monnàber Nou
Monnàber
Tel. +34 971 87 71 76
Menestralia
Palma-Sa Pobla Motorway. Exit 35
Tel. +34 971 51 67 37

DEIÀ
Ca'n Jaume
Arxiduc Lluis Salvador, 22
Tel. +34 971 63 90 29
Can Quet
Valldemossa road
Tel. +34 971 63 91 96

ESCORCA
Restaurant Escorca
Ses Cases, 2
Tel. +34 971 51 70 95

ESPORLES
Es Brollador
Psg. del Rei, 10
Tel. +34 971 61 05 39
Meson La Villa
Nou de Sant Pere, 5
Tel. +34 971 61 09 01

ESTELLENCS
Montimar
Pl. Constitució, 7
Tel. +34 971 61 85 76

FORNALUTX
Ca n'Antuna
Arbona-Colom, 14
Tel. +34 971 63 30 68
Es Turó
Arbona Colom, 4
Tel. +34 971 63 08 08

GALILEA
Cafè Sa Plaça
Pl. Pius XII, 1
Tel. +34 971 61 41 87

LLOSETA
Santi Taura
Església, 16
Tel. +34 971 54 46 22

LLUC (ESCORCA)
Sa Fonda
Sanctuary of Lluc
Tel. +34 971 51 70 22

MANCOR DE LA VALL
Ca'n Tiró Turixant
Bartomeu Reus, 21
Tel. +34 971 87 07 41

ORIENT
Orient
Alaró-Bunyola road, km 10.2
Tel. +34 971 61 51 53
Mandala
Nou, 1
Tel. +34 971 61 52 85

POLLENÇA
La Font del Gall
Montision, 4
Tel. +34 971 53 03 96
Can Costa
Costa i Llobera, 11
Tel. +34 971 53 12 76
La Llonja
Moll Vell.
Port de Pollença
Tel. +34 971 86 84 30

PUIGPUNYENT
Ses Cotxeries
Major, 8
Tel. +34 971 61 66 26

SANTA MARIA DEL CAMÍ
Celler Sa Font
Pl. Hostals, 14
Tel. +34 971 62 03 02
Celler Sa Sini
Pl. Hostals, 20
Tel. +34 971 62 02 52

SELVA
Ca's Teuler
Ctra. Inca–Selva, Km 3
Tel. +34 971 51 57 77

SÓLLER
Es Guia Castanyer, 2
Tel. +34 971 63 02 27
Sa Cova
Pl. Constitució, 7
Tel. +34 971 63 32 22
Es Canyís
Platja d'en Repic
Port de Sóller
Tel. +34 971 63 14 06
Mirador de ses Barques
Sóller-Lluc road, km 452
Tel. +34 971 63 07 92

VALLDEMOSSA
Ca'n Pedro
Av. Lluís Salvador
Tel. +34 971 61 21 70
Can Costa
Ctra. Valldemossa-Deià, km 2.5
Tel. +34 971 61 22 63
Cases de Cas Garriguer-Vistamar
Valldemossa-Deià road, km 2.5
Tel. +34 971 61 22 63
Es Port
Port de Valldemossa
Tel. +34 971 61 61 94

CELLARS FROM THE SERRA DE TRAMUNTANA
www.petitscellers.es

Winemaking in the Serra de Tramuntana dates back to the Roman period in *Pollentia* (Alcúdia today). Later, in the 14th century, important sea trading began, above all in the wines from Alcúdia. The phylloxera plague, in 1891, represented a disaster for the vineyards and cellars. Today, the effort and courage of the vine growers has enabled Mallorcan wines to once again occupy the place which, for tradition and quality, they so deserve.

The most outstanding varieties of red wine are the **Cabernet-Sauvignon**, the **Merlot** and the local **Mantell Negre**; the white varieties are the **Malmsey**, the **Chardonnay** and the Mallorcan **Moll**.

The reds have a deep colour and powerful tannins. The Malmsey whites are dry and fresh, with great aromatic strength, with a fruity predominance. The Chardonnay whites are pleasant and balanced, with a persistent aftertaste.

All over the Serra de Tramuntana you will find interesting cellars to visit.

ANDRATX
1 SANTA CATARINA
Tel. +34 971 23 54 13
www.santa-catarina.com

PUIGPUNYENT
2 SON PUIG
Tel. +34 971 61 41 84
www.sonpuig.com

ESTABLIMENTS (PALMA)
3 SON MAYOL
Tel. +34 871 60 00 26
www.bodegasonmayol.es

ESTELLENCS
4 TOMEU ISERN
Tel. +34 699 72 17 06
www.tomeuisern.es

ESPORLES
5 ES VERGER
Tel. +34 971 61 92 20
www.esverger.es
6 SON VICH DE SUPERNA
Tel. +34 629 03 89 49
www.sonvichdesuperna.es

BANYALBUFAR
7 CA'N PICÓ
Tel. +34 971 61 81 89
www.bodegacanpico.com
8 CELLER SON VIVES
Tel. +34 609 60 19 04
www.bodegasonvives.com
9 COOPERATIVA
DE SA MALVASIA
Tel. +34 616 53 71 46
www.malvasiadebanyalbufar.com

SANTA MARIA DEL CAMÍ
10 JAUME DE PUNTIRÓ
Tel. +34 971 62 00 23
www.vinsjaumedepuntiro.com
11 MACIÀ BATLE
Tel. +34 971 14 00 14
www.maciabatle.com
12 RAMANYÀ
Tel. +34 680 41 79 29
www.bodegaramanya.com
13 SEBASTIÀ PASTOR
Tel. +34 971 62 03 58
www.sebastiapastor.com

ANGEL
14 ANGEL
Tel. +34 971 18 01 18
www.bodegasangel.com
15 7103 PETIT CELLER
Tel. +34 644 23 89 58
Facebook: 7103 Petit Celler

CONSELL
16 BODEGUES RIBAS
Tel. +34 971 62 26 73
www.bodegaribas.com

ALARÓ
17 CASTELL MIQUEL
Tel. +34 971 51 06 98
www.castellmiquel.com
18 VINYES D'ALARÓ
Tel. +34 971 72 11 29
Facebook: Vinyes d'Alaró

BINISSALEM
19 VINS NADAL
Tel. +34 971 51 10 58
www.vinsnadal.es
20 JOSE L. FERRER
Tel. +34 971 51 10 50
www.vinosferrer.com
21 CA'N VERDURA
Tel. +34 695 81 70 38
Facebook: Vins Ca'n Verdura
22 SON CAMPANER
Tel. +34 618 59 62 33
www.soncampaner.es
23 BINIGUAL
Tel. +34 971 51 15 24
www.bodegabiniagual.com

SELVA
24 DIVINS CAN SERVERA
Tel. +34 651 55 59 45
www.divins.es

ESCORCA
25 VINYES MORTITX
Tel. +34 971 18 23 39
www.vinyesmortitx.com

POLLENÇA
26 CA'N VIDALET
Tel. +34 971 53 17 19
www.canvidalet.com
27 XALOC
Tel. +34 971 53 19 10
www.bodegasxaloc.com

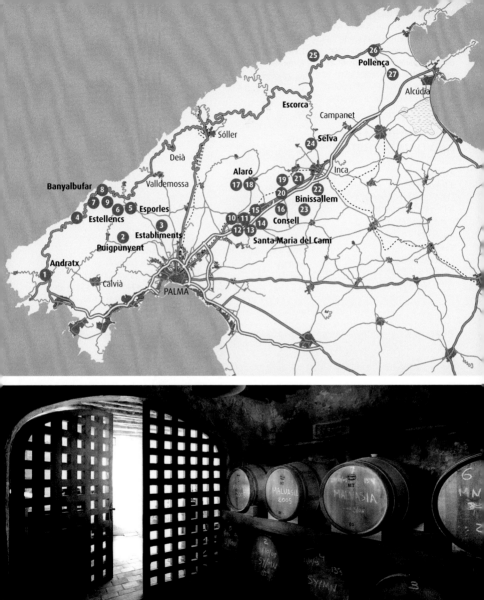

ACCOMMODATION

The area has all kinds of accommodation. Rural tourism, houses within towns (interior tourism), hostels and hotels of different categories that are dotted around the Serra de Tramuntana. The list includes some of the most interesting, well situated in urban centres or in the heart of nature.

RURAL TOURISM ^A
AND COUNTRY HOTELS^{HR}

ALARÓ
S'Olivaret ^{HR}
Alaró-Orient road, km 3
Tel. +34 971 51 08 89
www.solivaret.com

ANDRATX
Son Esteve ^A
Camí Cas Vidals, 42
Tel. +34 655 57 26 30
www.sonesteve.com

CALVIÀ
Son Malero ^A
Camí de Son Malero s/n
Tel. +34 971 67 03 01
www.sonmalero.es

CAMPANET
Monnàber Vell ^A
Afores, s/n
Tel. +34 971 51 61 31
www.monnabervell.com

DEIÀ
Sa Pedrissa ^{HR}
Valldemossa road, km 64,5
Tel. +34 971 63 91 11
www.sapedrissa.com

ESPORLES
Alfatx ^A
Valldemossa road, km 10,9
Tel. +34 971 61 79 46
www.agroturismo-alfatx.com

ORIENT
Son Palou ^A
Plaça de l'Església, s/n
Tel. +34 971 14 82 82
www.sonpalou.com

POLLENÇA
Son Sant Jordi ^{TI}
Sant Jordi, 29
Tel. +34 971 53 03 89
www.hotelsonsantjordi.com

PUIGPUNYENT
Son Burguet ^A
Palma-Puigpunyent road, km 10,8
Tel. +34 971 61 42 41
www.son-burguet.com

SANTA MARIA DEL CAMÍ
Es Molí de Son Maiol ^A
Camí de Marratxinet, s/n
Tel. +34 656 32 62 63
www.sonmaiol.com

SÓLLER
Ca n'Aí ^{HR}
Camí de Son Sales, 50
Tel. +34 971 63 24 94
www.canai.com

Ca's Curial ^A
Vilallonga, 21-23
Tel. +34 971 63 33 32
www.cascurial.com

VALLDEMOSSA
Son Brondo [A]
Palma-Valldemossa road, km 14,3
Tel. +34 971 61 22 58
www.fincasonbrondo.com
Cases de Cas Garriguer
Vistamar [HR]
Valldemossa-Andratx road
Tel. +34 971 61 23 00
www.casesdecasgarriguer.com
Mirabó [HR]
Valldemossa road, km 16
Tel. +34 661 28 52 15
www.mirabo.es

HOTELS AND
AND INTERIOR TOURISM[TI]

BANYALBUFAR
Mar i Vent ***
Major, 49
Tel. +34 971 61 80 00
www.hotelmarivent.com
Sa Baronia **
Baronia, 16
Tel. +34 971 61 81 46
www.hbaronia.com
DEIÀ
Es Molí ****
Valldemossa-Deià road
Tel. +34 971 63 90 00
www.esmoli.com
S'Hotel des Puig [TI]
Es Puig, 4
Tel. +34 971 63 94 09
www.hoteldespuig.com
ESTELLENCS
Maristel ****
Eusebi Pascual, 10
Tel. +34 971 61 85 50
www.hotelmaristel.com
LLUCALCARI
Hotel Costa d'Or ****
Llucalcari s/n
www.hoposa.es
Tel. +34 971 63 90 25

ORIENT
Dalt Muntanya ****
Bunyola-Orient road, km 10
Tel. +34 971 61 53 73
www.daltmuntanya.net
POLLENÇA
Posada de Lluc [TI]
Roser Vell, 11
Tel. +34 971 53 52 20
www.posadalluc.com
PORT D'ANDRATX
La Pérgola ****
Aparthotel
Av. S'Almudaina, 16
Tel. +34 971 67 15 50
www.hotelpergolamallor
ca.com
Mon Port Hotel&Spa ****
Cala d'Egos
Tel. +34 971 23 86 23
www.hotelmonport.com
PORT DE POLLENÇA
Llenaire [TI]
Camí de Llenaire, km 3,8
Tel. +34 971 53 52 51
www.hotelllenaire.com
Miramar ***
Pg. Anglada Camarasa, 39
Tel. +34 971 86 64 00
Tel. +34 971 86 72 11
www.hotel-miramar.net
PORT DE SÓLLER
Espléndido ***
Es Traves, 5
Tel. +34 971 63 18 50
www.esplendidohotel.com
Hotel Es Port ****
Antoni Montis s/n
Tel. +34 971 63 16 50
www.hotelesport.com
SELVA
Can Calco [TI]
Campanet, 1
Tel. +34 971 51 52 60
www.cancalco.com

SÓLLER
Salvia ****
De la Palma, 18
Tel. +34 971 63 49 36
www.hotelsalvia.com
La Vila [TI]
Plaça Constitució, 14
Tel. +34 971 63 46 41
www.lavilahotel.com
FORNALUTX
Can Reus [TI]
De l'Auba, 26
Tel. +34 971 63 11 74
www.canreushotel.com
Ca'n Verdera ****
Des Toros, 1
Tel. +34 971 63 82 03
www.canverdera.com

HOSTALS

ALARÓ
Can Tiú
Petit, 11
Tel. +34 971 86 23 43
www.hostalcantiumallorca.com
LLUC (ESCORCA)
Hospederia
Santuari de Lluc
Plaça dels Peregrins, 1
Tel. +34 971 87 15 25
www.lluc.net
(see page 107)
PORT D'ANDRATX
Catalina Vera
Isaac Peral, 63
Tel. +34 971 67 19 18
www.hostalcatalinavera.es

TRANSPORT

We can consult timetables and all information about public transport around the island at: http://tib.caib.es

or by calling **+34 971 17 77 77**

RAILWAY

The Mallorca Railway Services **(SFM)** and the Sóller Railway are at the interchange station of Plaça d'Espanya, in the **Parc de ses Estacions**, (c/ Eusebi Estada), in Palma.

RAILWAY LINES

To reach the towns of **Santa Maria del Camí, Alaró, y Lloseta**, (in the Serra de Tramuntana area) we must use the **SFM** line:

Palma | Marratxí | Inca | Manacor | Sa Pobla

SÓLLER RAILWAY

The journey takes place on a charming electric train with wooden carriages that passes through tunnels and viaducts. The landscape that can be enjoyed from the train is at its best splendour during the month of February, when the almond trees are in bloom. The tourist trains also stop at the **Pujol d'en Banya** viewpoint where there is a beautiful panorama of the Sóller valley. Once in Sóller, there is the possibility of going to the **Port of Sóller** on an old and very special tram that passes through orange and lemon groves. For more information we can consult: www.trendesoller.com

BUS

The Illes Balears bus station **(TIB)** is also in the **Parc de ses Estacions**, in Palma. Bus transport around the island is organised in 5 zones that cover the whole island. The Serra de Tramuntana zone is covered by the **L100, L200** and **L300** lines. Lines **L400** and **L500** cover the rest of the island.

100 LINES

L100 Andratx | Port d'Andratx | S'Arracó | Sant Elm

L102 Palma | Santa Ponça | Peguera | Andratx | Port d'Andratx

L103 Palma | Portals | Son Caliu | Santa Ponça | Peguera

L104 Palma | Portals | Son Caliu | Palmanova | Magaluf | Santa Ponça | Costa de la Calma | Peguera

L105 Palma | Palmanova | Magaluf | El Toro | Son Ferrer

L106 Palma | Son Caliu | Portals | Magaluf | Palmanova

L107 Palma | Son Caliu | Marineland | Magaluf | Palmanova | Casino | Cala Vinyes

L111 Palma | Portals Platja | Portals Son Caliu | Son Bugadelles | Calvià | Es Capdellà

L140 Palma | Puigpunyent | Galilea

200 LINES

L200 Palma | Esporles | Banyalbufar | Estellencs

L210 Platja de Palma | Palma | Valldemossa | Deià | Llucalcari | Sóller | Port de Sóller

L211 Palma | Palmanyola | Bunyola | Sóller | Port de Sóller

L212 Sóller | S'Horta de Biniaraix | Fornalutx

L220 Palma | Palmanyola | Hospital Joan March | Pla de sa Coma | Bunyola

L221 Bunyola | Orient

300 LINES

We only mention the **L300** buses that connect the towns in the Serra de Tramuntana zone.

L301 Estació Marratxí | Festival Park | Sa Cabaneta | Pòrtol

L302 Estació Pont d'Inca Nou | Ses cases Noves | Can Carbonell | Cas Capità | Pla de na Tesa | Can Baló | Pont d'Inca | Nova Cabana | Son Macià | Es Garrovers | Son Daviu

L311 Estació Santa Maria | Santa Eugènia | Ses Alqueries | Biniali | Sencelles

L312 Estació Inca | Sencelles | Costitx

L320 Estació Alaró/Consell | Alaró

L330 Palma | Festival Park | Santa Maria | Consell | Binissalem | Lloseta | Inca | Selva | Caimari | Lluc

L331 Estació Inca | Mancor | Biniamar

L332 Estació Inca | Selva | Moscari | Lluc

L333 Estació Inca | Campanet | Búger

L340 Palma | Inca | Pollença | Port de Pollença | Llenaire | Club del Sol

L341 Estació Inca | Pollença | Club del Sol

L342 Estació Sa Pobla | Pollença | Port de Pollença | Llenaire | Club del Sol Palma | Port de Pollença | Palma

L352 Port de Pollença | Alcúdia | Port d'Alcúdia | Can Picafort

Sóller

Pollença

Alcúdia

Badia d'Alcúdia

Zona 2

Valldemossa

Zona 3

Inca

sa Pobla

Artà

Zona 1

PALMA

Sineu

Zona 4

Manacor

Andratx

Portocristo

Badia de Palma

Llucmajor

Felanitx

Portocolom

Zona 5

Santanyí

Portopetro

Cap Blanc

Cala Santanyí

Distribution of bus lines on the island and Tren de Sóller route

HEALTHCARE
www.ibsalut.es

EMERGENCIES
Tel. 112

HOSPITALS

PALMA
Hospital de la Creu Roja
Pons i Gallarza, 50
Tel. +34 971 75 14 45
Hospital General
Plaça Hospital, 3
Tel. +34 971 21 20 00
Hospital Joan March
Bunyola road, km 12,5
Tel. +34 971 21 22 00
Hospital Sant Joan de Déu
Passeig Cala Gamba, 53
Tel. +34 971 26 58 54
**Hospital Universitari
Son Espases**
Valldemossa, 79
Tel. +34 871 20 50 00
Hospital Son Llàtzer
Manacor road, km 4
Tel. +34 871 20 20 00

INCA
Hospital Comarcal d'Inca
Llubí old road, s/n
Tel. +34 971 88 85 00

MANACOR
Hospital de Manacor
Manacor-Alcúdia road, s/n
Tel. +34 971 84 70 00

HEALTH CENTRES

ANDRATX
C.S. Can Riera
Bernat Riera, 65
Tel. +34 971 13 67 81
Tel. +34 971 23 57 29

CALVIÀ
C.S. Santa Ponça
Riu Sil, 25
Tel. +34 971 69 46 54

POLLENÇA
C.S. Pollença
Bisbe Desbach, s/n
Tel. +34 971 53 23 01

SÓLLER
C.S. Serra Nord
Camí Camp Llarg, 18
Tel. +34 971 63 30 11

GESMA
Mallorca Healthcare Service
Emergencies 061

RED CROSS
Tel. +34 971 29 50 00
Emergencies Tel. +34 971 20 22 22

PHARMACIES
www.cofib.es

© **Triangle Postals SL**
Sant Lluís, Menorca
Tel. +34 971 15 04 51
www.triangle.cat

Text
Gaspar Valero, Imma Planas

Photography
Biel Puig, Biel Santandreu, Jaume Serrat, Sebastià Mas, Sebastià Torrens, Laia Moreno, Oleguer Farriol: Ricard Pla, Hans Hansen, Jordi Puig, Jordi Todó, Gaspar Valero, Pedro Castell, Joan Oliva, Pere Vivas, Carmen Vila, Juanjo Puente, Hugo Arenella, Aina Pla, Joan Colomer, Toni Darder, Oriol Aleu.

Graphic design
Joan Colomer

Layout
Vador Minobis

Translation
Nicholas Nabokov

Illustrations
Leonard Beard

Cartography
Joan Esteve, Triangle Postals

Printed in Barcelona, 05-2018

Registration number: B-25022-2009

ISBN: 978-84-8478-401-2